Teach Yourself VISUALLY™

Photoshop® CS6

Visual™

Mike Wooldridge
Brianna Stuart

WILEY

John Wiley & Sons, Inc.

Teach Yourself VISUALLY™ Photoshop® CS6

Published by
John Wiley & Sons, Inc.
10475 Crosspoint Boulevard
Indianapolis, IN 46256

www.wiley.com

Published simultaneously in Canada

Library of Congress Control Number: 2012939588

ISBN 978-1-118-19667-0

Manufactured in the United States of America

10 9 8 7 6 5 4 3 2 1

Trademark Acknowledgments

Contact Us

For general information on our other products and services please contact our Customer Care Department within the U.S. at 877-762-2974, outside the U.S. at 317-572-3993 or fax 317-572-4002.

For technical support please visit www.wiley.com/techsupport.

WILEY **Sales** | Contact Wiley at (877) 762-2974 or fax (317) 572-4002.

Credits

Senior Acquisitions Editor
Stephanie McComb

Project Editor
Terri Edwards

Technical Editor
Dennis Cohen

Copy Editor
Scott Tullis

Editorial Director
Robyn Siesky

Business Manager
Amy Knies

Senior Marketing Manager
Sandy Smith

Vice President and Executive Group Publisher
Richard Swadley

Vice President and Executive Publisher
Barry Pruett

Project Coordinator
Sheree Montgomery

Graphics and Production Specialists
Ronda David-Burroughs
Jennifer Mayberry
Jill Proll

Quality Control Technician
John Greenough

Proofreading and Indexing
Debbye Butler
Potomac Indexing, LLC

Vertical Websites Project Manager
Rich Graves

Vertical Websites Associate Producer
Rich Graves

About the Authors

Mike Wooldridge is a writer and web developer based in the San Francisco Bay Area. He has authored dozens of books for the Visual series. For more information about him and his books, visit www.wooldridge.net.

Brianna Stuart is an author and busy mom based in the Seattle area. She is also the author of *Teach Yourself Visually Photoshop Elements 10* and *Creating Web Pages Simplified*.

Authors' Acknowledgments

Mike and **Brianna** thank Terri Edwards, Scott Tullis, Dennis Cohen, and everyone else at Wiley for their help on this book. Mike dedicates this book to his wonderful wife and son, who also love digital photography. Brianna thanks her wonderful extended work family for their support and good humor, even when they are repeatedly subjected to her silly image editing hijinks. She dedicates this book, with lots of love and giggles, to the goofiest twins in the world: Beckett and Owain.

How to Use This Book

Who This Book Is For

This book is for the reader who has never used this particular technology or software application. It is also for readers who want to expand their knowledge.

The Conventions in This Book

❶ Steps

This book uses a step-by-step format to guide you easily through each task. **Numbered steps** are actions you must do; **bulleted steps** clarify a point, step, or optional feature; and **indented steps** give you the result.

❷ Notes

Notes give additional information — special conditions that may occur during an operation, a situation that you want to avoid, or a cross-reference to a related area of the book.

❸ Icons and Buttons

Icons and buttons show you exactly what you need to click to perform a step.

❹ Tips

Tips offer additional information, including warnings and shortcuts.

❺ Bold

Bold type shows command names or options that you must click or text or numbers you must type.

❻ Italics

Italic type introduces and defines a new term.

Table of Contents

Chapter 3   Changing the Size of an Image

Chapter 4   Making Selections

Table of Contents

Chapter 7   Adjusting Lighting and Colors

Table of Contents

Chapter 9   Applying Layer Styles

Chapter 10   Applying Filters

Table of Contents

CHAPTER 1

Getting Started

Are you interested in creating, modifying, combining, and/or optimizing digital images on your computer? This chapter introduces you to Adobe Photoshop CS6, a popular software application for working with digital images.

Work with Images

Photoshop is a popular photo-editing program you can use to modify, optimize, and organize digital images. You can use the program to make imperfect snapshots clearer and more colorful, as well as retouch and restore older photos. With layers, you can isolate objects in your images and apply special effects just to those objects, or combine multiple images into a collage. After you are finished editing your photos, you can save the images to print, share via e-mail, publish online, or view on a mobile device or tablet.

Manipulate Photos

As its name suggests, Photoshop excels at editing digital photographs. The program includes numerous image-editing tools and commands you can apply to manipulate the look of your photos. Whether you import photos from a digital camera or a scanner, you can apply a wide variety of editing techniques to your images, from subtle adjustments in color to elaborate filters that make your snapshots look like paintings. See Chapter 7 for more on adjusting color and Chapter 10 for more on filters.

Paint Pictures

Photoshop's painting features make it a formidable illustration tool as well as a photo editor. You can apply colors or patterns to your images with a variety of brush styles. See Chapter 6 for more on applying color. In addition, you can use the program's typographic tools to integrate stylized letters and words into your images. See Chapter 12 for more on type. You can also create geometric shapes, which are covered in Chapter 11.

Create a Digital Collage

You can combine different image elements in Photoshop. Your compositions can include photos, scanned art, text, and anything else you can save on your computer as a digital image. By placing elements in Photoshop onto separate layers, you can move, transform, and customize them independently of one another. See Chapter 8 for more on layers. You can also merge several side-by-side scenes into a seamless panorama, which is covered in Chapter 13.

Access, Organize, and Display Photos

Photoshop's Bridge interface offers an easy-to-use tool to access and preview images stored on your computer. See the section "Browse for an Image in Bridge." With Bridge, you can easily tag your images with descriptive information, such as where or when they were taken. You can then use that information to sort your photos. Photoshop also offers useful ways to display your images after you edit them. You can display them as a group in a web photo gallery or combine them on a printed page as a contact sheet. See Chapter 13 for more.

Put Your Images to Work

After you edit your work, you can utilize your images in a variety of ways. Photoshop enables you to print your images, save them in a format suitable for placement on a web page or e-mailing, or prepare them for use in a page-layout program. By using the program's optimization settings, you can ensure that your image files are small in size but still look good. See Chapter 14 for more on saving images in different formats, as well as printing them.

daisy.gif

digital_art.jpg

mbadventure.png

windsurfing_boards.jpg

Understanding Photoshop

Photoshop's tools enable you to move, color, stylize, and add text to your images. You can optimize the contrast and lighting in photographs or turn them into interesting works of art by applying filters.

Understanding Pixels

Digital images in Photoshop consist of tiny, solid-color squares called *pixels*. Photoshop works its magic by rearranging and recoloring these squares. You can edit specific pixels or groups of pixels by selecting the area of the photo you want to edit. If you zoom in close, you can see the pixels that make up your image. For more on the Zoom tool, see Chapter 2.

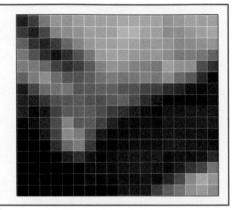

Choose Your Pixels

To edit specific pixels in your image, you must first select them by using one of Photoshop's selection tools. You can make geometric selections by using the marquee tools or free-form selections by using the Lasso tool. See Chapter 4 for more on the selection tools. Photoshop also has a number of commands that help you select specific parts of your image, such as a certain color or range of colors. Special brushes in Photoshop enable you to select objects in your image based on how the colors of those objects contrast with the background.

Paint

After selecting your pixels, you can apply color to them by using Photoshop's Brush, Mixer Brush, Paint Bucket, and Pencil tools. You can also fill your selections with solid or semitransparent colors, patterns, or pixels copied from another part of your image. Painting is covered in Chapter 6. Special painting tools help you seamlessly cover up objects in your image or eliminate dust specks, tears, and other imperfections from a scanned picture.

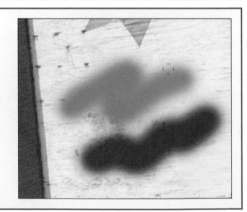

Adjust Color

You can brighten, darken, and change the hue of colors in parts of your image with Photoshop's Dodge, Burn, and similar tools. Other commands display interactive dialog boxes that let you make wholesale color adjustments so you can correct overly dark or light digital photographs. See Chapter 7 for more. You can also add adjustment layers to your image that enable you to make changes to the color commands later on. See Chapter 8 for more about layers.

Apply Styles and Filters

Photoshop's layer styles let you easily add drop shadows, frame borders, and other effects to your images. You can also perform complex color manipulations or distortions by using filters. Filters can make your image look like an impressionist painting, sharpen or blur your image, or distort your image in various ways. Chapters 9 and 10 cover styles and filters.

Add Text

Photoshop's type tools make it easy to apply titles and labels to your images. With the Character and Paragraph panels, you can control the size, spacing, and alignment of your text. You can combine these tools with the program's special effects commands to create warped, 3-D, or wildly colored words and characters. You can learn more about adding text in Chapter 12.

Start Photoshop on a PC

Afterfter you install Photoshop, you can start it to begin creating and editing digital images. Common ways of obtaining and installing the program include from DVD disc or by downloading it from Adobe over the Internet. On a PC, you can access Photoshop as you do other programs — through the Start menu.

Start Photoshop on a PC

1 Click the **Start** button.

2 Click **All Programs** (All Programs changes to Back).

3 Click **Adobe Photoshop CS6**.

Note: Your path to the Photoshop program may be different depending on how you installed your software.

Photoshop starts.

Note: To learn how to open an image and start working, see the section "Open an Image."

Start Photoshop on a Mac

After you install Photoshop, you can start it to begin creating and editing digital images. Common ways of obtaining and installing the program include from DVD disc or by downloading it from Adobe over the Internet. On a Mac, you can access Photoshop through the Finder in the Applications folder or by using the LaunchBar.

Start Photoshop on a Mac

1 In the Finder, click **Applications**.

2 Click the **Adobe Photoshop CS6** folder.

3 Double-click **Adobe Photoshop CS6**.

Note: The exact location of the Adobe Photoshop icon may be different depending on how you installed your software.

Photoshop starts.

Note: To learn how to open an image and start working, see the section "Open an Image."

The Photoshop Workspace

In Photoshop, you open your digital images in a main image window and then use a combination of tools, menu commands, and panel-based features to edit the images.

Ⓐ Application Bar

Displays menus that contain most of Photoshop's commands and functions.

Ⓑ Options Bar

Displays controls that let you customize the selected tool in the Toolbox.

Ⓒ Title Tab

Displays the name, magnification, and color mode of an open image. You can switch between images by clicking their respective tabs.

Ⓓ Image Window

Displays the images you open in Photoshop.

Ⓔ Toolbox

Displays a variety of icons, each one representing an image-editing tool. You click and drag inside your image to apply most of the tools. Also displays the current foreground and background colors.

Ⓕ Status Bar

Displays the magnification of the current image and the amount of computer memory that image is using.

Ⓖ Panels

Small windows that give you access to common commands and resources. You can click the tabs and icons to display and hide panels.

Find Images for Your Projects

You can get raw material to work with in Photoshop from a variety of sources.

Start from Scratch

You can create your Photoshop image from scratch by opening a blank canvas in the image window. Then, you can apply color and patterns with Photoshop's painting tools or cut and paste parts of other images to create a composite. See the section "Create a New Image" for more on opening a blank canvas.

Digital Camera Photos

Digital cameras are a great way to get digital images onto your computer. Most digital cameras save their images in JPEG, TIFF, or RAW format, all of which you can open and edit in Photoshop. The program's color adjustment tools, covered in Chapter 7, are great for correcting color and exposure flaws in digital camera images.

Scanned Photos and Art

A scanner gives you an inexpensive way to convert existing paper- or slide-based content into digital form. You can scan photos and art into your computer, retouch and stylize them in Photoshop, and then output them to a color printer. To automatically separate photos that were scanned together as a single image, see Chapter 3.

Affordable Online Photos

There are many websites that feature images that are in the public domain or are available for noncommercial use. Wikimedia Commons (http://commons.wikimedia.org) is one such site. If you have a little money to spend, you can license images from *microstock* websites, which are known for low-cost, downloadable images. iStockphoto (http://www.istockphoto.com) is a popular microstock site.

Set Preferences

Photoshop's Preferences dialog boxes enable you to change default settings and customize how the program looks. You can set preferences to create a workspace that matches how you like to work.

When you make changes to the program in the preferences, the changes remain after you exit the program and then open it again.

Set Preferences

1. Click **Edit** (**Photoshop** on a Mac).
2. Click **Preferences**.
3. Click **General**.

The Preferences dialog box opens and displays General options.

4. Click here (☐) to select which dialog box opens when you select a color.
5. Select the general options you want to use (☐ changes to ☑).
6. Click **Interface**.

The Interface options appear.

7 Click to select a color theme.

A You can select from menus (▼) to further customize the interface colors.

8 You can click check boxes to customize the behavior of menus, panels, and other interface features (☐ changes to ☑).

9 Click **Units & Rulers**.

The Units & Rulers options appear.

10 Click here (▼) to select the units for the window rulers.

These units become the default units selected when you resize an image.

11 Click here (▼) to select the default units for type.

12 Click **OK**.

Photoshop sets preferences to your specifications.

What type of measurement units should I use in Photoshop?

You should use the units most applicable to the type of output you intend to produce. Pixel units are useful for web imaging because monitor dimensions are measured in pixels. Inches, centimeters, and picas are useful for print because those are standards for working on paper. You can set this under the Units & Rulers preferences.

How can I change the number of operations saved in the History panel?

You can backtrack through your work by using the History panel. To change the number of operations Photoshop remembers, click **Performance** in the Preferences window and then change the History States value. Photoshop can remember as many as 1,000 operations. The default is 20.

Save a Workspace

You can position the different Photoshop panels, define keyboard shortcuts, customize your menus, and then save the arrangement as a workspace. This can be helpful if you work on various types of Photoshop projects that require the use of different tools and commands. You can access the different workspaces that you have saved under the Window menu.

Save a Workspace

Save a Workspace

1 Arrange the Toolbox and panels in the Photoshop interface.

To define keyboard shortcuts or customize menus, click **Edit** and then **Keyboard Shortcuts** or **Menus**.

2 Click **Window**.

3 Click **Workspace**.

4 Click **New Workspace**.

14

The New Workspace dialog box opens.

5 Type a name for your workspace.

6 Select the interface elements you want to save (☐ changes to ☑).

7 Click **Save**.

Photoshop saves the workspace.

Select a Workspace

1 Click **Window**.

2 Click **Workspace**.

3 Click a workspace.

You can choose a workspace you have defined previously or one of Photoshop's predefined workspaces.

Photoshop rearranges the workspace.

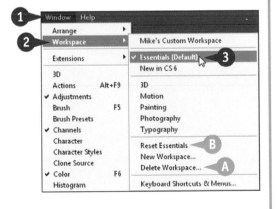

TIP

How do I return to the default workspace?

Follow these steps:

1 Click **Window**.

2 Click **Workspace**.

3 Click **Essentials (Default)**.

Photoshop returns you to the default setup, with the Toolbox on the left side and panels on the right.

Ⓐ You can click **Delete Workspace** to get rid of a workspace you have saved.

Ⓑ You can click the **Reset** command to return the currently selected workspace to its original arrangement.

Open an Image

You can open an image in Photoshop to modify it or to use it in a project. After you open the photo, you can adjust its color and lighting, add special effects, and move objects in the photo to separate layers.

You can open more than one photo at a time. You can switch between photos using the title tabs. For information about managing images after you open them, see Chapter 2.

Open an Image

1 Click **File**.

2 Click **Open**.

The Open dialog box appears.

3 Click here (▪) to choose the type of files to display in the window.

All Formats is the default and displays all image and nonimage formats.

④ Click here (▣) to browse to the folder that contains the image you want to open.

⑤ Click the image you want to open.

⑥ Click **Open**.

Photoshop opens the image in a window.

Ⓐ The filename appears in a title tab.

You can specify that images open in floating windows rather than with tabs in the Interface preferences.

Note: For more on preferences, see the section "Set Preferences."

How do I open a recently accessed image?

① Click **File**.

② Click **Open Recent**.

A list of recently opened files appears.

③ Click the image's filename.

Photoshop opens the image.

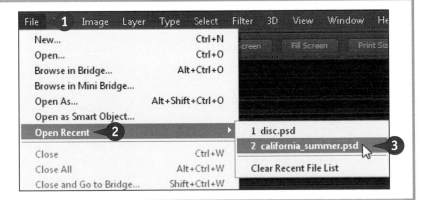

Browse for an Image in Bridge

You can open an existing image file by using the Adobe Bridge file browser. Bridge offers a user-friendly way to find and open your images.

In Bridge, you can also add descriptive information to your images and sort them. See the tasks that follow in this chapter for more information.

Browse for an Image in Bridge

1 Click **File**.

2 Click **Browse in Bridge**.

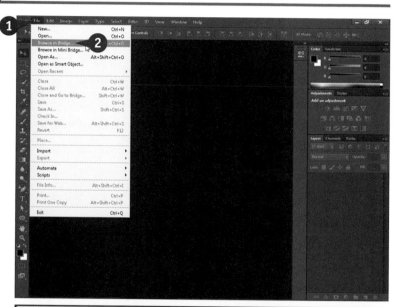

The Adobe Bridge file browser opens.

3 Click the **Folders** tab.

4 Click ▶ to open folders on your computer (▶ changes to ▼).

5 Click a folder on your computer to browse.

The folders and files inside the folder appear.

6 Click an image.

A A preview and information about the image appear.

In this example, the right panel has been widened slightly to show more image information.

7 Double-click the image file to open it.

The image opens in Photoshop.

How do I add a rating or label to an image in Bridge?

In Bridge, click the image, click **Label**, and then click a star rating or color label. You can apply a rating from one to five stars or a text label such as "approve" or "reject." Applying ratings or labels to your images enables you to sort them by rating or label in the Bridge interface. See the section "Sort and Filter Images in Bridge" for more.

How can I easily access my image folders in Bridge?

You can mark particular folders where you store your images as favorites in Bridge. To access the Favorites list, click the Favorites tab in the top left corner of Bridge. To mark a folder as a favorite, click the folder on the right side of the Bridge window and then drag it to the Favorites list. A name and icon for that folder appear.

Sort and Filter Images in Bridge

You can sort your images by filename, date, file size, dimensions, and other characteristics in Bridge. This can be helpful when you are dealing with hundreds or thousands of images in a collection and need to find a particular image quickly. You can also filter the information displayed in Bridge, specifying that it show only images with a particular rating or label.

Sort and Filter Images in Bridge

Sort Images

1 Open Adobe Bridge.

2 Click a folder to display its contents.

Note: For more, see the section "Browse for an Image in Bridge."

3 Click **View**.

4 Click **Sort**.

5 Click a category by which to sort.

Bridge sorts the images.

Ⓐ You can also sort images by using the Sort By menu.

Filter Images

1 Click a category by which to filter your images (■ changes to ■).

Photoshop displays filter options for the category.

Note: For more on applying ratings, labels, and other categories, see the section "Browse for an Image in Bridge."

2 Click a filter option.

Bridge filters the images, hiding irrelevant ones.

B A check mark appears next to the clicked filter option.

C You can filter by a rating by clicking **Filter Items by Rating** (■).

TIPS

How can I hide folders and nonimage files in Bridge so that only images appear?

To hide folders, click **View** and then **Show Folders**. The check mark next to the Show Folders menu item disappears, and Bridge hides the folders in the right side of the window. To also hide nonimage files, click **View** and then **Show Graphic Files Only**.

What image-editing functions can I perform in Bridge?

You can rotate images 90 degrees by clicking ■ (rotate counterclockwise) or ■ (rotate clockwise). You can delete images by selecting them and clicking ■. To perform more complex editing, you can return to Photoshop by clicking **File** and then **Return to Adobe Photoshop CS6**.

Display a Slide Show in Bridge

You can view a set of images in a folder as a slide show in Adobe Bridge. You can control the cycling of the slide show images by using keyboard commands.

Display a Slide Show in Bridge

① Open Adobe Bridge.

② Click a folder containing the slide show images.

Note: For more, see the section "Browse for an Image in Bridge."

③ Click **View**.

④ Click **Slideshow Options**.

The Slideshow Options dialog box opens.

You can specify the duration between slides, alignment, and other settings.

⑤ Click **Play** to open the first slide.

Note: On a Mac, the position of the Play and Done buttons is reversed in the Slideshow Options dialog box.

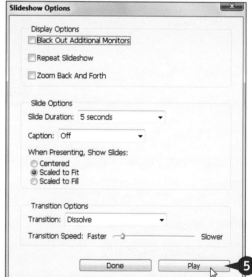

Bridge starts the slide show and cycles through the photos in the selected folder.

Ⓐ You can press Spacebar to pause and resume the slide show.

The sort order in Bridge determines the order of the photos.

Note: See the section "Sort and Filter Images in Bridge" for more.

❻ Press H.

Ⓑ Bridge displays the slide show keyboard commands.

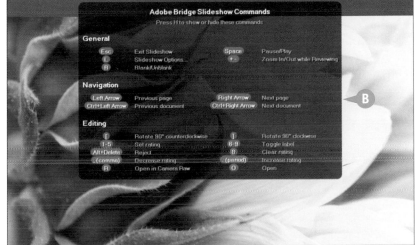

❼ Press Esc.

The slide show ends.

How can I group similar images in Bridge?

You can group similar images by creating a stack.

❶ Ctrl +click to select the images you want to stack.

❷ Click **Stacks**.

❸ Click **Group as Stack**.

Photoshop creates a single thumbnail for the stack and displays the number of images in the stack.

You can click the number to reveal the stacked images.

Import Images from a Camera in Bridge

Y ou can import images from a digital camera into a folder on your computer using Photoshop. After the import, you can browse and manage the images in Bridge and open them in Photoshop for editing. Most cameras today connect to a computer through a USB port. A typical PC or Mac comes with multiple USB ports. Make sure the device is properly connected before you begin.

On most Macs, the default behavior when connecting a camera is to import photos into iPhoto. You can change this behavior in the iPhoto preferences.

Import Images from a Camera in Bridge

1 Open Adobe Bridge.

Note: For more, see the section "Browse for an Image in Bridge."

2 Click **Get Photos from Camera** icon (![icon]).

The Photo Downloader dialog box appears.

3 Click the down arrow (![arrow]) to choose your camera.

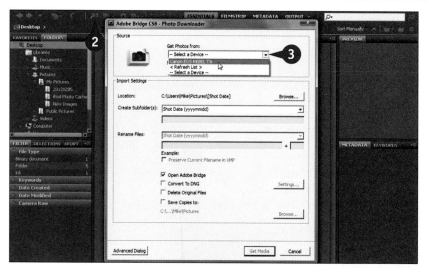

By default, Bridge downloads your photos into dated subfolders inside your Pictures folder. The dated subfolders are based on the time stamp associated with each photo.

A You can click **Browse** to select a different download location.

B You can click the ![arrow] to choose a different naming scheme for the subfolders.

4 Click the ![arrow] to choose a naming scheme for your files.

C Click here to delete the photos from the camera after downloading.

D You can click here to save copies of the imported files to another location (☐ changes to ☑). This can be useful for archiving.

5 Click **Get Media**.

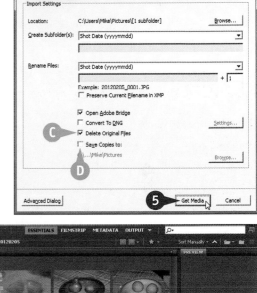

Bridge downloads the photos from the camera.

E To view them, select the download location under the Folders tab.

Note: For more information, see "Browse for an Image in Bridge."

TIP

How do I use the Advanced dialog box in the Photo Downloader?

1 Click **Advanced Dialog** in the bottom left corner of the Photo Downloader.

A All photos are selected and downloaded by default. You can click here to deselect a photo.

B Click here to apply metadata to the images such as copyright and creator information (☐ changes to ☑).

2 Click **Get Media**.

Create a New Image

Y ou can start a Photoshop project by creating a blank image and then adding photographic, textual, and other content to the blank image. When you create a blank image, you specify the dimensions and the resolution. Photoshop offers a number of useful preset sizes, including common paper sizes. For more about choosing a resolution, see Chapter 3.

You can add content from other images to your blank image as separate layers. For more on layers, see Chapter 8. You can also use the Brush tool to add streaks of color. See Chapter 6 for information about using and customizing the Brush.

Create a New Image

1 Click **File**.

2 Click **New**.

The New dialog box opens.

3 Type a name for the new image.

Ⓐ You can click here (⯆) to choose a preset image size.

4 Type the dimensions and resolution you want.

Note: For more on dimensions and resolution, see Chapter 3.

5 Click **OK**.

Photoshop creates a new image window at the specified dimensions.

Ⓑ The image name appears in the title tab.

6 Use Photoshop's tools and commands to create your image.

Note: To learn how to save your image, see Chapter 14.

Exit Photoshop

You can exit Photoshop after you finish using the application. Before exiting, Photoshop alerts you to any open images that have unsaved changes so you can save them.

When you start the application again, it opens with the same Toolbox and panel arrangement as you had when you exited. For more about customizing a workspace, see "Save a Workspace."

Exit Photoshop

Exit Photoshop on a PC

1 Click **File**.

2 Click **Exit**.

Photoshop closes.

Before exiting, Photoshop alerts you to any open images that have unsaved changes so you can save them.

Note: See Chapter 14 to learn how to save image files.

Exit Photoshop on a Mac

1 Click **Photoshop**.

2 Click **Quit Photoshop**.

Photoshop closes.

Before exiting, Photoshop alerts you to any open images that have unsaved changes so you can save them.

Note: See Chapter 14 to learn how to save image files.

CHAPTER 2

Understanding Photoshop Basics

Are you ready to start working with images? This chapter shows you how to select tools and fine-tune your workspace. You can also undo commands or revert an image when you make a mistake and want to start over.

Introducing the Photoshop Toolbox

Photoshop offers a variety of specialized tools that enable you to edit your image. Take some time to familiarize yourself with the Toolbox tools.

You can select tools by clicking buttons in the Toolbox or by typing a keyboard shortcut key. Keyboard shortcut keys are shown in parentheses.

Ⓐ Move (V)

Moves selected areas of an image.

Ⓑ Marquee (M)

Selects pixels by drawing a box or ellipse around the area you want to edit.

Ⓒ Lasso (L)

Selects pixels by drawing a free-form shape around the area you want to edit.

Ⓓ Quick Selection Brush (W)

Selects pixels with brush shapes.

Ⓔ Crop (C)

Trims an image to create a new size.

Ⓕ Eyedropper (I)

Samples color from an area of an image.

Ⓖ Spot Healing Brush (J)

Quickly fixes slight imperfections by cloning nearby pixels.

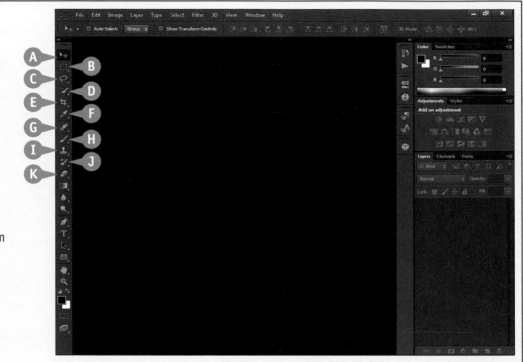

Ⓗ Brush (B)

Paints strokes of color.

Ⓘ Clone Stamp (S)

Duplicates an area of the image.

Ⓙ History Brush (Y)

Paints a previous state of your image onto the current image.

Ⓚ Eraser (E)

Erases pixels.

Ⓐ Gradient (G)

Fills selected areas with blended color effects.

Ⓑ Blur (R)

Blurs objects in your image.

Ⓒ Dodge (O)

Brightens specific areas of your image.

Ⓓ Pen (P)

Creates custom shapes by drawing and connecting lines or paths.

Ⓔ Type (T)

Adds type to an image or selects type that you have added.

Ⓕ Path Selection (A)

Selects lines that you have drawn with the pen or other tools.

Ⓖ Rectangle (U)

Draws solid, rectangular shapes.

Ⓗ Hand (H)

Shifts an image in the image window to display unseen parts.

Ⓘ Zoom (Z)

Zooms your view of an image in or out.

Ⓙ Foreground and Background Colors

Displays and lets you set foreground and background colors.

Hidden Tools

Tool buttons that include a small triangle (■) in the corner have hidden tools located beneath them. Click and hold a tool button to access the hidden tools. You can also right-click a tool to access additional tools. For example, the Lasso has a Polygonal Lasso and a Magnetic Lasso hidden beneath it. You can cycle through hidden tools beneath a tool by repeatedly typing the shortcut key for that tool.

Work with Toolbox Tools

You can use the tools in Photoshop's Toolbox to make changes to an image. Positioning the mouse pointer over a tool displays the tool name. After you click to select a tool, the Options bar displays controls for customizing the tool. Some tools include a small triangle (⊤) in the corner to indicate hidden tools.

Work with Toolbox Tools

Select a Tool

1 Position the mouse pointer (↖) over a tool.

A A label appears displaying the tool name and the tool's shortcut key, if it has one.

2 Click a tool.

The Options bar displays customizing options for the selected tool.

3 Specify any options you want for the tool.

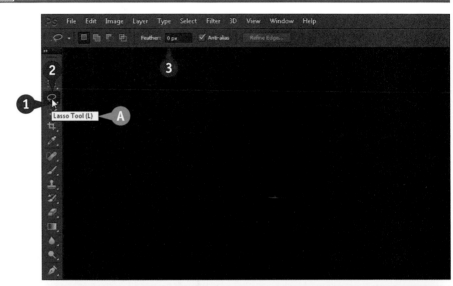

Select a Hidden Tool

1 Click a tool that has a triangle (⊤) in its corner.

2 Press and hold the mouse button.

Note: You can also right-click the tool.

A menu of hidden tools appears.

3 Click the tool you want to use.

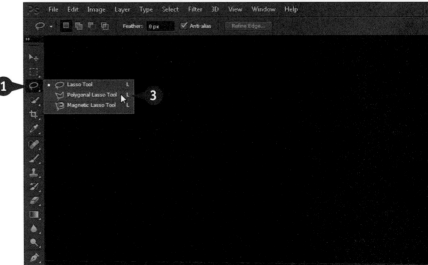

Rearrange the Toolbox

1 Click 🔛.

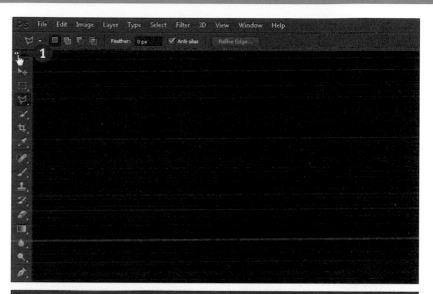

B Photoshop rearranges the Toolbox tools into two columns.

C You can click 🔙 to switch back to a single column.

TIPS

How do I float the Toolbox?
You can float the Toolbox to drag it to a more convenient place on the screen. To float the Toolbox, click and drag the title bar of the Toolbox. You can unfloat the Toolbox by dragging it back to near the left edge of the screen. When you release the mouse button, Photoshop snaps the Toolbox to the left edge.

How do I close the Toolbox?
Closing the Toolbox frees up space in the Photoshop interface. To close the Toolbox, click **Window** and then click **Tools**. To reopen the Toolbox, click **Window** and then click **Tools** again. You can also press **Tab** to open or close the Toolbox as well as all panels. Items that are open in the workspace have check marks next to them in the Window menu.

Magnify with the Zoom Tool

You can change the magnification of an image with the Zoom tool. With this tool, you can view small details in an image or view an image at full size. Zooming in on an image can be helpful when selecting complex areas of your image or retouching small areas. Zooming out gives you a view of a project's overall composition.

If you zoom in very close, you can see the square, solid-color pixels that make up your image.

Magnify with the Zoom Tool

Increase Magnification

1 Click the **Zoom** tool ( ).

   changes to .

2 Click the image.

Photoshop increases the magnification of the image.

You can also press Ctrl + = to zoom in (⌘ + = on a Mac).

The point that you clicked in the image is centered in the window.

A The current magnification shows in the title tab and status bar.

B You can choose an exact magnification by typing a percentage value in the status bar.

Decrease Magnification

1 Click the **Zoom Out** icon (🔍).

ᴉ changes to 🔍.

2 Click the image.

Photoshop decreases the magnification.

You can also press **Ctrl**+**-** to zoom out (**⌘**+**-** on a Mac).

C The current magnification shows in the title bar and status bar.

You can also press and hold **Alt** (**Option** on a Mac) and then click the image to decrease magnification.

Use Scrubby Zoom

1 Click the Scrubby Zoom check box (☐ changes to ☑).

Scrubbing means moving within a multimedia file to find an area of interest.

2 Click and drag with the 🔍.

Photoshop zooms as you drag.

3 Release the mouse button.

Photoshop magnifies the image.

TIP

How do I quickly return an image to 100% magnification?

1 Double-click the **Zoom** tool (🔍).

2 Click **Actual Pixels** on the Options bar.

3 Click **View** and then click **Actual Pixels** from the menu.

4 Type **100%** in the corner of the image window.

5 Right-click the image and then choose **Actual Pixels**.

6 Press **Ctrl**+**1** (**⌘**+**1** on a Mac).

Adjust Views

You can move an image within the window by using the Hand tool or scroll bars. The Hand tool helps you navigate to an exact area of an image that has been magnified. The tool is especially useful for examining details in very large images.

The Hand tool is a more flexible alternative to using the scroll bars because, unlike the scroll bars, the Hand tool enables you to drag the image freely in two dimensions.

Adjust Views

Using the Hand Tool

1 Click the **Hand** tool ().

    changes to .

Note: For the Hand tool to produce an effect, the image must extend outside the boundary of the image window.

2 Click **Window**.

3 Click **Navigator**.

Ⓐ The Navigator panel opens to show your current view relative to the entire image.

4 Click and drag inside the image window.

The view of the image shifts inside the window.

B The Navigator panel shows the changed view.

Using the Scroll Bars

1 Click and hold one of the window's scroll bar buttons (■, ■, ■, or ■).

The image scrolls.

Note: On a Mac with OS X Lion, you can scroll by clicking and dragging scroll bars.

TIP

How can I quickly adjust the image window to see the entire image at its largest possible magnification on-screen?

Here are 5 ways to magnify the image to its largest possible size:

1 Double-click the **Hand** tool (■).

2 Click **Fit Screen** on the Options bar.

3 Click **View** and then click **Fit on Screen** from the menu.

4 Right-click the image and then choose **Fit on Screen**.

5 Press Ctrl+0 (⌘+0 on a Mac).

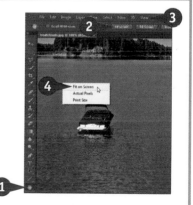

Change Screen Modes

You can switch the screen mode to change the look of your workspace on-screen and give yourself more room to view your current image. Activating Full screen mode removes the Toolbox, panels, and other interface elements and displays your image on a clean, black background.

In the Standard screen mode, you can view multiple images at the same time, each in a different window. For more on viewing open images, see the section "Manage Image Windows."

Change Screen Modes

Switch to Full Screen Mode with Menu Bar

1 Click **View**.

2 Click **Screen Mode**.

3 Click **Full Screen Mode With Menu Bar**.

Photoshop hides the title tabs, status bar, and other features to increase the amount of space you have to work with.

If you have multiple images open, you can switch between them in the Window menu.

Switch to Full Screen Mode

1 Click **View**.

2 Click **Screen Mode**.

3 Click **Full Screen Mode**.

4 If a dialog box opens explaining Full screen mode, click **Full Screen** to close it.

The image appears full screen without the application bar, Options bar, Toolbox, or panels.

You can press **F** or **Esc** to return to Standard screen mode.

You can press **Tab** or move your cursor to the sides of the screen to open the Toolbox and panels.

Note: Pressing **Tab** hides the Toolbox and panels in all of Photoshop's screen modes.

TIPS

Is there a shortcut for changing screen modes?

Press **F** to cycle through the screen modes by using your keyboard. To cycle through in opposite order, press **Shift**+**F**. You can also exit Full screen mode by pressing **Esc**.

How do I change tools while in Full screen mode?

You can open the Toolbox by pressing **Tab**, or you can press a shortcut key. Below are shortcut keys for the more popular tools. For a complete list, see the section "Introducing the Photoshop Toolbox."

Marquee	**M**	Type	**T**
Move	**V**	Zoom	**Z**
Lasso	**L**	Eraser	**E**
Brush	**B**	Quick Selection tool	**W**

Using Rulers and Guides

You can turn on rulers and create guides to help place elements accurately in your image. Rulers appear on the top and left sides of your image with a unit of measure that is configurable in your preferences. See Chapter 1 for details about setting preferences for Photoshop.

Guides are straight lines parallel to the rulers that can help you align elements in your image with one another. These lines do not appear on a printed image.

Using Rulers and Guides

View Rulers and Guides

1 Click **View**.

2 Click **Rulers**.

Note: To change the units of measurement on rulers and make other preference changes, see Chapter 1.

Ⓐ Photoshop adds rulers to the top and left sides of the image window.

3 Click one of the rulers and then drag the cursor into the window (▷ changes to ↔).

You can drag the top ruler down to create a horizontal guide.

You can drag the left ruler to the right to create a vertical guide.

B A thin, colored line called a *guide* appears.

You can also click **View** and then click **New Guide** to add a guide.

To hide and show guides in your image, click **View**, **Show**, and then **Guides**.

Move a Guide

1 Click the **Move** tool (⊕).

2 Position your cursor over a guide (⬚ changes to ⟷).

3 Click the guide and then drag it to a new position.

TIP

How do I make objects in my images "snap to" my guides when I move those objects?

You can use the "snap to" feature when you want to align layer elements in a row (horizontally) or in a column (vertically).

1 Click **View**.

2 Click **Snap To**.

3 Click **Guides**.

Photoshop places a check mark next to Guides.

A When you move an object, Photoshop automatically snaps it to any nearby guides.

Undo Commands

You can undo multiple commands by using the History panel. This enables you to correct mistakes or change your mind about operations you have performed on your image. The History panel lists recently executed commands, with the most recent command at the bottom. Clicking a command returns the image to the state the image was in when the command was executed.

You can specify how many commands Photoshop remembers in the History panel in the preferences. For details about setting preferences, see Chapter 1.

Undo Commands

1 Click **Window**.

2 Click **History**.

The History panel opens, listing commands previously applied to the image.

3 Click a previous command.

Ⓐ Photoshop returns the image to the previous state.

Ⓑ You can click a later command in the menu to redo commands.

Revert an Image

You can revert an image to the previously saved state and then begin editing your image again. This can be useful when you are unhappy with the edits you have made and you want to start over.

If you just want to undo a few specific commands, you can choose which ones to revert using the History panel. See "Undo Commands" for details.

Revert an Image

1 Click **File**.

2 Click **Revert**.

Photoshop reverts the image to its previously saved state.

You can click **Edit** and then click **Undo Revert** to return to the unreverted state.

Manage Image Windows

Each image you open in Photoshop appears in its own window. Windows can take up the entire workspace, and you can select between different ones by clicking tabs. You can also float or tile windows so you can see content from more than one window at once. This can be useful if you are copying content between them.

For other ways to manage the look and feel of your Photoshop workspace, see "Change Screen Modes."

Manage Image Windows

1 Open two or more images.

Note: For more on opening images, see Chapter 1.

A The active, or current, image appears here.

By default, the different open images are distinguished by tabs.

2 Click the tab for the image you want to view.

You can also select your images from a list at the bottom of the Window menu.

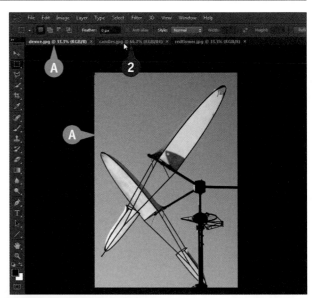

B The image you select appears as the active image.

3 Click **Window**.

4 Click **Arrange**.

5 Click **Float in Window**.

C Photoshop displays the active image in a floating window.

You can click and drag the title bar to move the window.

6 Click **Window**.

7 Click **Arrange**.

8 Click **Tile**.

Photoshop tiles the windows so that all images are visible.

D You can click and drag here to resize the window.

Note: To copy content between two open windows, see Chapter 5.

You can click **Window** and then click **Consolidate All to Tabs** to return the windows to tabs.

TIPS

How can I make the views consistent between different open images?

You can click **Window**, **Arrange**, and then **Match Zoom** to set the zoom levels of all the open images to that of the active image. You can click **Window**, **Arrange**, and then **Match Location** to make the viewing location consistent across all open images. To match both zoom and location, click **Window**, **Arrange**, and then **Match All**.

Are there shortcuts for managing tabbed windows?

Yes. You can right-click a window's tab to access a menu of commands. The commands include Close for closing that tab's image, Close All for closing all the currently open images, and Open Document for opening a new image.

CHAPTER 3

Changing the Size of an Image

You can change the size of your image to make it fit on a web page or in a printed document. This chapter shows you how to change the on-screen size, print size, and print resolution, as well as how to crop an image.

Change the On-Screen Size of an Image

You can change the on-screen size of an image you are working with in Photoshop to make it better fit the confines of your monitor. Shrinking an image can also lower its file size and make it easier to share via e-mail or on the web.

When you change an image's on-screen size, Photoshop resamples the image. *Resampling* is the process of increasing or decreasing the number of pixels in an image. Enlarging or shrinking an image too much can cause a noticeable decrease in image quality, which you can notice by examining details using the Zoom tool.

Change the On-Screen Size of an Image

① Click **Image**.

② Click **Image Size**.

Ⓐ The Image Size dialog box opens, listing the height and width of the image.

③ Make sure **Resample Image** is selected (■ changes to ☑) to change the number of pixels in the image.

Changing the number of pixels changes the on-screen size.

④ Type a size for a dimension.

Ⓑ To resize by a certain percentage, click here (▾) to change the units to percent. Changing the units of one menu automatically changes the units of the other.

Ⓒ Click the **Constrain Proportions** check box (■ changes to ☑), if it is not already selected, to force the other dimension to change proportionally.

Ⓓ You can restore the original dialog box settings by pressing and holding Alt (Option on a Mac) and then clicking **Cancel**, which changes to **Reset**.

⑤ Click **OK**.

Photoshop resizes the image.

Note: Increasing the number of pixels in an image can add blur. To sharpen a resized image, apply the Unsharp Mask filter, as covered in Chapter 10.

TIP

How do I change the size of an image as I am saving it for the web?

Follow these steps:

① Click **File** and then **Save for Web**.

The Save for Web dialog box opens.

② Type a new value in the W or H field to change the dimensions of your image.

③ Click **Save** to save the resized image.

Note: For more on saving images for the web, see Chapter 14.

Change the Print Size of an Image

You can change the printed size of an image to determine how it appears on paper. Print size is also called *document size* in Photoshop. If you change the print size of an image with the Resample Image option checked, Photoshop adjusts the number of pixels in the image but keeps the resolution the same. If the resampling option is unchecked, the resolution changes but not the number of pixels. Photoshop also gives you resizing options when you print your image. For more about printing, see Chapter 14.

Change the Print Size of an Image

1 Click **Image**.

2 Click **Image Size**.

A The Image Size dialog box opens, listing the current height and width of the printed image.

B You can click here (▼) to change the unit of measurement.

3 Type a size for a dimension.

C You can click the **Constrain Proportions** check box (☐ changes to ☑), if not already selected, to force the other dimension to change proportionally.

D You can restore the original dialog box settings by pressing and holding **Alt** (**Option** on a Mac) and then clicking **Cancel**, which changes to **Reset**.

4 Click **OK**.

Photoshop resizes the image.

Note: Changing the number of pixels in an image can add blur. To sharpen a resized image, apply the Unsharp Mask filter, as covered in Chapter 10.

TIP

How do I preview an image's printed size?
Follow these steps:

1 Click **File** and then **Print**.

A A dialog box displays how the image will print on the page.

B Other options enable you to adjust the size and positioning of the image.

Note: For more on printing images, see Chapter 14.

Change the Resolution of an Image

You can change the print resolution of an image to increase or decrease the print quality. The resolution, combined with the number of pixels in an image, determines the size of a printed image. The greater the resolution, the better the image appears on the printed page — up to a limit, which varies with the type of printer you use and the paper on which you are printing.

For more about how Photoshop determines the size of images, see "Change the On-Screen Size of an Image" and "Change the Print Size of an Image."

Change the Resolution of an Image

1 Click **Image**.

2 Click **Image Size**.

Ⓐ The Image Size dialog box opens, listing the current resolution of the image.

3 Make sure **Resample Image** is selected (■ changes to ☑) to change the number of pixels in the image as you adjust the resolution.

Ⓑ You can click here (▾) to change the resolution units.

④ Type a new resolution.

ⓒ You can restore the original dialog box settings by pressing and holding **Alt** (**Option** on a Mac) and then clicking **Cancel**, which changes to **Reset**.

⑤ Click **OK**.

In this example, adjusting the resolution changes the number of pixels in the image. The on-screen image becomes larger or smaller, whereas the print size stays the same.

TIPS

What is the relationship between resolution, on-screen size, and print size?

To determine the printed size of a Photoshop image, you can divide the on-screen size by the resolution. If you have an image with an on-screen width of 480 pixels and a resolution of 120 pixels per inch, the printed width is 4 inches.

How can I use the Ruler tool (📏) to measure dimensions in my image?

Click and hold the **Eyedropper** tool (🖊) and then click the **Ruler** tool (📏). You can then click and drag inside your image to measure the dimensions of objects. Click **Window** and then **Info** to open the Info panel and see your measurements. You can change the Info panel units in the Units & Rulers preferences. See Chapter 1 for more on changing preferences.

Crop an Image

You can use the Crop tool to quickly remove unneeded space on the top, bottom, and sides of an image. Cropping is a great way to edit out unwanted background elements. You can also rotate the cropping boundary prior to cropping, which enables you to rotate while you are cropping.

You can also crop an image by changing its canvas size. For more information, see the section "Change the Canvas Size of an Image." Another way is by selecting an area with a selection tool, clicking **Image**, and then clicking **Crop**. See Chapter 4 for more on making selections.

Crop an Image

Crop Only

1 Click the **Crop** tool (⬚).

⬚ changes to □.

2 Click and drag □ to select the area of the image you want to keep.

You can also crop an image by changing its canvas size or by using a selection tool, such as the Rectangular Marquee tool (▤), and then clicking **Image** and then **Crop**.

Note: See the section "Change the Canvas Size of an Image" for more.

3 Click and drag the side and corner handles (□) to adjust the size of the cropping boundary.

Ⓐ You can click here (▤) to show or hide guides in the tool. You can choose **Rule of Thirds** to add pairs of horizontal and vertical lines to help line up objects in the image.

Ⓑ To exit without cropping the image, you can click ⊘ or press Esc to cancel.

4 To accept the crop, click ✓ or press Enter (⌘+Return on a Mac).

Photoshop crops the image,
deleting the pixels outside
the cropping boundary.

Rotate and Crop

1 Perform steps **1** to **3** under
"Crop Only."

2 Click and drag outside the
boundary lines.

3 To accept, click ☑ or press
Enter (⌘+Return on a
Mac).

Photoshop rotates the image
and crops it.

<hr>

TIP

How can I constrain the dimensions of the Crop tool?
Follow these steps:

1 Type the width and height of the cropping boundary on
the Options bar.

2 Drag ☐ to apply the Crop tool.

Photoshop constrains the rectangle to the specified
dimensions.

Crop and Straighten Photos

You can automatically crop and straighten one or more photographs in a Photoshop image. After you finish cropping and straightening the images, Photoshop places each image in its own image window. This feature is useful if you digitize several images at the same time on a scanner and want to separate them.

The feature works best when the images to be cropped and straightened contrast with the background. This is usually the case when you digitize images on a scanner.

Crop and Straighten Photos

① Click **File**.

② Click **Automate**.

③ Click **Crop and Straighten Photos**.

Ⓐ Photoshop straightens the photos, crops out any blank space, and copies the photos to separate image windows.

Note: For more on saving newly cropped images, see Chapter 14.

Ⓑ The original image remains in its own window.

Trim an Image

You can use the Trim command to automatically remove any blank space surrounding your image. This can be useful for scanned photos or when you want to minimize the file size of an image. Options enable you to trim space from all four sides or just some of them.

The feature works best when the image to be trimmed contrasts with the background. Trimming is a way to automate what you commonly do with the Crop tool. See "Crop an Image" for more details.

Trim an Image

1 Click **Image**.

2 Click **Trim**.

The Trim dialog box opens.

3 Specify how to select the type of pixels you want to trim (◎ changes to ◉).

4 Select the areas to trim (■ changes to ☑).

5 Click **OK**.

Photoshop trims the image.

Ⓐ The Trim command can sometimes leave extra space around the image. You can use the Crop tool to remove it. See "Crop an Image" for details.

Change the Canvas Size of an Image

You can alter the canvas size of an image to change its rectangular shape or add space around its borders. The canvas is the area on which an image sits. Changing the canvas size is one way to crop an image or add *matting*, which is blank space, around an image.

Photoshop warns you when you decrease the dimensions of the image canvas because this deletes part of the image. You might want to increase the canvas size if you are adding images to make a collage and want the images to overlap one another.

Change the Canvas Size of an Image

1 Click **Image**.

2 Click **Canvas Size**.

Ⓐ The Canvas Size dialog box opens, listing the current dimensions of the canvas.

Ⓑ You can click here (▪) to change the unit of measurement.

58

③ Type the new canvas
dimensions.

Ⓒ You can modify in what
directions Photoshop
changes the canvas size by
clicking an anchor point.

Ⓓ You can specify the color
with which Photoshop fills
any new canvas area if you
enlarge a dimension.

④ Click **OK**.

Note: If you decrease a dimension,
Photoshop displays a dialog box
asking whether you want to proceed.
Click **Proceed**.

Photoshop changes the image's
canvas size.

Because the middle anchor point
is selected in this example, the
canvas size changes equally on
opposite sides.

TIPS

**How do I increase the area of an image by using
the Crop tool?**

You can enlarge the image window to add extra
space around the image. Then, you can apply the
Crop tool (🔲) so the cropping boundary extends
beyond the borders of the image. When you apply
cropping, the image canvas enlarges. Photoshop
applies the current background color in the new
space. For more on selecting colors, see Chapter 6.

**How can I crop without making the image canvas
smaller?**

Use a selection tool, such as the Rectangular
Marquee tool (▦), to select a cropping boundary.
Click **Select** and then **Inverse** to select the area
outside the boundary. Pressing `Backspace` (`Del`
on a Mac) crops the image but keeps your canvas
dimensions the same. If you are working with a
multilayer image, this technique crops content only
in the selected layer.

CHAPTER 4

Making Selections

You can move, color, or transform parts of your image independently from the rest of the image. The first step is to make a selection. This chapter shows you how to use the Photoshop selection tools to isolate portions of your images for editing. You can use different tools to select objects in your image or areas of similar color.

Select with the Marquee Tools

You can select parts of an image for editing by using a marquee. You can then make changes to the selected area by using other Photoshop commands.

Two marquee tools are available: The Rectangular Marquee enables you to select rectangular shapes, including squares, and the Elliptical Marquee enables you to select elliptical shapes, including circles. You click and drag diagonally in your image to apply both tools. You can also use settings in the Options bar to define specific dimensions for your marquees such as a fixed size or ratio.

Select with the Marquee Tools

Using the Rectangular Marquee Tool

① Click the **Rectangular Marquee** tool (▦).

⬦ changes to +.

② Click and drag diagonally inside the image window.

You can press and hold Shift while you click and drag to create a square selection.

Ⓐ Photoshop selects a rectangular portion of your image. You can now perform other commands on the selection.

Ⓑ You can deselect a selection by clicking **Select** and then **Deselect**.

Using the Elliptical Marquee Tool

1 Click and hold the **Rectangular Marquee** tool (▣).

2 In the list that appears, click the **Elliptical Marquee** tool (◉).

   ⬚ changes to +.

3 Click and drag diagonally inside the image window.

You can press and hold Shift while you click and drag to create a circular selection and then press Alt (Option on a Mac) to draw the circle directly out from the center.

C Photoshop selects an elliptical portion of your image. You can now perform other commands on the selection.

D You can deselect a selection by clicking **Select** and then **Deselect**.

TIP

How do I customize the marquee tools?
Use the settings on the Options bar.

A *Feather:* The Feather value softens your selection edge, which means that Photoshop partially selects pixels near the edge.

B *Style:* Define your marquee tool as a fixed size or fixed aspect ratio.

C *Height and Width:* Add an exact width and height for a fixed-size selection or a ratio for a fixed-aspect-ratio selection by typing values in the Width and Height boxes.

Select with the Lasso Tool

You can create irregularly shaped selections with the lasso tools. You can then make changes to the selected area by using other Photoshop commands. Which lasso you use depends on the shapes and edges of the objects in your image that you want to select.

You can use the regular Lasso tool to create freehand selections. The Polygonal Lasso tool enables you to easily create a selection bounded by many straight lines. To select objects with well-defined edges, you can use the Magnetic Lasso tool, which is covered in "Select with the Magnetic Lasso Tool."

Select with the Lasso Tool

Using the Regular Lasso

1 Click the **Lasso** tool (⬭).

2 Click and drag your cursor (⬭) to make a selection.

Ⓐ To accurately trace a complicated edge, you can magnify that part of the image with the Zoom tool (🔍).

Note: See Chapter 2 for more on the Zoom tool.

3 Drag to the beginning point and then release the mouse button.

The selection is complete.

Using the Polygonal Lasso

1 Click and hold the **Lasso** tool ().

2 Click the **Polygonal Lasso** tool (⬚) in the list that appears.

    ↘ changes to ⋎.

3 Click multiple times along the border of the area you want to select.

4 To complete the selection, click the starting point.

You can also double-click anywhere in the image and Photoshop adds a final straight line connected to the starting point.

The selection is complete.

You can achieve a polygonal effect with the regular Lasso tool by pressing `Alt` (`Option` on a Mac) and then clicking to make your selection.

TIP

What if my lasso selection is not as precise as I want it to be?

Selecting complicated outlines with ⬚ can be difficult, even for the steadiest of hands. To fix an imprecise Lasso selection, you can:

- Deselect the selection by clicking **Select** and then **Deselect** and then trying again.
- Try to fix your selection. See the section "Add to or Subtract from a Selection."
- Switch to the Magnetic Lasso tool (⬚). See the section "Select with the Magnetic Lasso Tool."

Select with the Magnetic Lasso Tool

You can quickly and easily select elements of your image that have well-defined edges by using the Magnetic Lasso tool. The Magnetic Lasso works best when the element you are trying to select contrasts sharply with its background. Some examples of good candidates for the tool include a bird in flight against a clear blue sky or a dark object against a light-colored wall.

As you drag the Magnetic Lasso along an edge, Photoshop places anchor points along the edge that fix the selection outline. You can press the Delete key to remove the anchor points as you draw to redraw the selection.

Select with the Magnetic Lasso Tool

1 Click and hold the **Lasso** tool.

2 Click the **Magnetic Lasso** tool (🔲) in the list that appears.

🔲 changes to 🔲.

3 Click the edge of the object you want to select.

This creates a beginning anchor point, which is a fixed point on the lasso path.

4 Drag your cursor (🔲) along the edge of the object.

The Magnetic Lasso's path snaps to the edge of the element as you drag.

A To help guide the lasso, you can click to add anchor points as you go along the path.

You can press Del to remove the most recently added anchor point. This allows you to restructure an incorrect lasso path.

5 Click the beginning anchor point to finish your selection.

Alternatively, you can double-click anywhere in the image and Photoshop completes the selection for you.

The path is complete.

This example shows that the Magnetic Lasso is less useful for selecting areas where you find little contrast between the image and its background.

TIP

How can I adjust the precision of the Magnetic Lasso tool?

You can use the Options bar to adjust the Magnetic Lasso tool's precision:

A *Width:* The number of nearby pixels the lasso considers when creating a selection.

B *Contrast:* How much contrast is required for the lasso to consider something an edge.

C *Frequency:* How often anchor points appear.

Width: 10 px   Contrast: 10%   Frequency: 57
A   **B**   **C**

Select with the Quick Selection Tool

You can paint selections onto your images by using the Quick Selection tool. The tool automatically expands the area you paint over to include similar colors and textures. This tool offers a quick way to select objects that have solid colors and well-defined edges. You can control the size and hardness of the tool, similarly to how you define the characteristics of the Brush tool. This determines how much area the tool selects as well as the softness of the selection edges.

Select with the Quick Selection Tool

1 Click the **Quick Selection** tool (🖌).

2 Click here (▾) to open the tool's Brush menu.

The Brush menu opens.

In the Brush menu, you can specify the tool's size and other characteristics. Decreasing the tool's hardness causes it to partially select pixels along the perimeter.

3 Click and drag inside the object you want to select.

Ⓐ Photoshop selects parts of the object based on its coloring and the contrast of its edges.

Ⓑ After you make a selection, the Add to Selection button (🖼) becomes active.

④ Click and drag to select more of the object.

Ⓒ Photoshop adds to the selection.

TIP

How can I adjust the selection made with the Quick Selection tool?

① On the Options bar, click **Refine Edge**.

The Refine Edge dialog box opens, and Photoshop turns the unselected part of your image white.

Ⓐ You can increase Feather to make the edges of

your selection partially transparent.

Ⓑ You can increase Contrast to heighten the sharpness of the selection edges.

Ⓒ You can use Shift Edge to move the selection in or out slightly.

Select with the Magic Wand Tool

You can select groups of similarly colored pixels with the Magic Wand tool. You may find this useful if you want to remove an object from a background. The tool is especially handy for selecting a clear sky, a green lawn, or white sand at a beach.

By specifying an appropriate tolerance value, you can control how similar a pixel needs to be for Photoshop to select it. The Tolerance value for the tool can range from 0 to 255, with smaller numbers causing the tool to select a narrower range of colors.

Select with the Magic Wand Tool

1 Click and hold the **Quick Selection** tool (▧).

2 Click the **Magic Wand** tool (▧).

⬚ changes to ✳.

3 Type a number from 0 to 255 in the Tolerance field.

To select a narrow range of colors, type a small number; to select a wide range of colors, type a large number.

4 Click the cursor (✳) in the area you want to select inside the image.

Photoshop selects the pixel you clicked plus any similarly colored pixels near it.

5 To add to your selection, press **Shift** and then click elsewhere in the image.

A You can also click the **Add to Selection** button (⊞) on the Options bar.

B You can click the **Subtract from Selection** button (⊟) to configure the Magic Wand to remove selected pixels.

C Photoshop adds to your selection.

Note: For more about editing a selection, see the section "Add to or Subtract from a Selection."

TIP

How can I ensure that the Magic Wand tool selects all the occurrences of a color in an image?
You can deselect the **Contiguous** check box (☑ changes to ◼) on the Options bar so the Magic Wand tool selects similar colors, even when they are not contiguous with the pixel you click with the tool. This can be useful when objects intersect the solid-color areas of your image. You can also click the **Sample All Layers** check box (◼ changes to ☑) to select similar colors in all layers in the image, not just the currently selected layer.

Select with the Color Range Command

You can select a set range of colors within an image with the Color Range command. With this command, you can quickly select a region of relatively solid color, such as a sky or a wall.

You select a range of colors in two steps. First you click inside the image to specify an initial color. Then you click and drag the Fuzziness slider to control what similar colors you also want to select. Photoshop selects the colors and displays them graphically in a Color Range dialog box.

Select with the Color Range Command

1 Click **Select**.

2 Click **Color Range**.

The Color Range dialog box opens.

⬚ changes to ⬚.

3 Click inside the image window.

Ⓐ Photoshop selects all the pixels in the image similar to the pixel you clicked. These areas turn white in the Color Range window.

Ⓑ The number of pixels that turn white depends on the Fuzziness setting.

4 To increase the range of color, click and drag the **Fuzziness** slider () to the right.

You can decrease the color range by dragging to the left.

C You can broaden the selected area by clicking the **Add to Sample** icon (🖌) and then clicking other parts of the image.

5 Click **OK**.

Photoshop makes the selection in the main image window.

Note: Sometimes, the Color Range command selects unwanted areas of the image. To eliminate these areas, see the section "Add to or Subtract from a Selection."

TIPS

How do I limit the area of the image that the Color Range command affects?
Select an area of the image — by using the Marquee, Lasso, or another tool — before clicking **Select** and then **Color Range**.

How do I select only contiguous similar colors in my image?
The Color Range command selects colors throughout your image, not just contiguous ones. To select a contiguous range of colors — for example, an isolated patch of grass — you can use the Magic Wand with the Contiguous setting selected. See "Select with the Magic Wand Tool" for more.

Select All the Pixels in an Image

You can select all the pixels in a single-layer image by using the Select All command. With the entire image window selected, you can easily delete the image or copy and paste it into another window.

For multilayer images, Select All selects all the pixels in the currently selected layer. To merge multiple layers into a single layer so that all the content in the image can be selected, see Chapter 8.

Select All the Pixels in an Image

1 Click **Select**.

2 Click **All**.

You can also press Ctrl+A (⌘+A on a Mac) to select all the pixels.

A Photoshop selects the entire image window.

You can delete the currently selected pixels by pressing Del.

To copy your image, press Ctrl+C (⌘+C on a Mac).

To paste your image, press Ctrl+V (⌘+V on a Mac).

Move a Selection Border

You can move a selection border if your original selection is not in the intended place. You can also move a selection border if you want to fill that area with content in a different part of your image.

Moving a selection border is different from moving the object selected by the border. For details about moving a selected object, see Chapter 5.

Move a Selection Border

1 Make a selection by using one of Photoshop's selection tools (+, ☉, or ✷).

A Make sure the New Selection button (▣) is highlighted.

2 Click and drag inside the selection.

B The selection border moves.

To move your selection border one pixel at a time, you can use the arrow keys on your keyboard.

You can hide a selection outline by clicking **View**, **Show**, and then **Selection Edges**.

Add to or Subtract from a Selection

You can add to or subtract from your selection by using various selection tool options. Adding enables you to select a large object in your image by making multiple selections. By subtracting, you can fix a selection that includes extraneous pixels.

Most selection tools have add and subtract settings in the Options bar. You can also create a selection using one selection tool and then add to or subtract from the selection using other tools. See the other sections in this chapter to learn how to choose the appropriate tool for selecting elements in your photo.

Add to or Subtract from a Selection

Add to a Selection

1 Make a selection by using one of Photoshop's selection tools (+, ▨, or ▨).

2 Click a selection tool.

This example uses the Magnetic Lasso tool (▨).

Note: See the previous sections in this chapter to select the appropriate tool for your image.

3 Click the **Add to Selection** button (▨).

4 Select the area you want to add.

5 Complete the selection.

Ⓐ Photoshop adds to the selection.

You can enlarge the selection further by repeating steps **2** to **5**.

You can also add to a selection by pressing Shift as you make your selection.

To select an intersection, press Shift + Alt (Shift + Option on a Mac) as you make your selection.

Subtract from a Selection

1 Make a selection by using one of Photoshop's selection tools.

2 Click a selection tool.

This example uses the Elliptical Marquee tool (⬭).

3 Click the **Subtract from Selection** button (◩).

4 Select the area you want to subtract.

R Photoshop deselects, or subtracts, the selected area.

You can subtract other parts of the selection by repeating steps **2** to **4**.

You can also subtract from a selection by pressing and holding **Alt** (**Option** on a Mac) as you make your selection.

TIPS

How do I add to or subtract from a selection by using the Quick Selection tool?

The Quick Selection tool features different option buttons for adding to or subtracting from a selection. On the Options bar, you can click ◪ to add to a selection and ◪ to subtract from a selection.

How can I expand or contract a selection?

To expand a selection, click **Select**, **Modify**, and then **Expand**. A dialog box opens, enabling you to specify the amount of expansion in pixels. To contract a selection, click **Select**, **Modify**, and then **Contract**. You can also expand and contract via the Refine Edge dialog box. See "Select with the Quick Selection Tool" for details.

Invert a Selection

You can invert a selection to deselect what is currently selected and select everything else. This is useful when you want to select the background around an object. You can select the object with one of the Photoshop selection tools and then perform the invert command to switch the selection to the background.

The inverted selection has the same characteristics as your initial selection. For example, if the initial selection has a feathered edge, the inverted result will also have a feathered edge. For more information about selecting objects, see the other sections in this chapter.

Invert a Selection

① Make a selection by using one of Photoshop's selection tools (+, ⬭, or 🔺).

Note: For more on the various selection tools, see the previous sections in this chapter.

② Click **Select**.

③ Click **Inverse**.

Photoshop inverts the selection.

Grow a Selection

You can increase the size of your selection by using the Grow command, which is useful when you want to include similarly colored, neighboring pixels. For example, if you select a sky with the Magic Wand and some areas with slightly different colors were left unselected, you can use the Grow command to finish the job.

The amount that the Grow command selects is controlled by the Tolerance setting for the Magic Wand tool. You can select the Magic Wand tool first to adjust that setting before executing the Grow command. See "Select with the Magic Wand Tool" for more.

Grow a Selection

1 Make a selection by using one of Photoshop's selection tools (+, 🔾, or 🔨).

Note: For more on the various selection tools, see the previous sections in this chapter.

2 Click **Select**.

3 Click **Grow**.

A The selection grows to include similarly colored pixels contiguous with the current selection.

B To also include noncontiguous pixels, you can click **Select** and then **Similar**.

C You can change the number of similarly colored pixels the Grow command selects by selecting the Magic Wand tool (🔨) and changing the Tolerance setting.

Create Slices

You can divide a large image that you want to display on the web into smaller rectangular sections called *slices*. The different slices of an image can then be optimized independently of one another for faster download.

For example, photographic slices in a sliced image can be saved in the JPEG format, whereas solid-color graphics can be saved in the PNG or GIF format. When you save a sliced image, Photoshop creates a separate HTML file that assembles the slices as a single web page. See Chapter 14 for more.

Create Slices

① Click and hold the **Crop** tool (⬛).

② Click the **Slice** tool (✂) in the list that appears.

  ▷ changes to ✎.

③ Click and drag inside the image to create a slice.

Ⓐ Photoshop creates a slice where you clicked and dragged.

Note: Slices you define are called *user slices*.

  Photoshop fills in the rest of the image with auto slices.

Note: User slices remain fixed when you add more slices to your image, whereas auto slices can change size.

④ Click and drag to define another slice in your image.

Ⓑ Photoshop creates another slice where you click and drag.

Photoshop creates or rearranges auto slices to fill in the rest of the image.

Note: For more on how to save the different slices for the web, see Chapter 14.

Note: To save a sliced image so you can edit the slices later, save the image in the Photoshop format. See Chapter 14 for more.

TIP

How do I resize or delete slices in my image?
First, click the **Slice Select** tool (), which you access by clicking and holding the Slice tool (). To resize a user slice, click inside it and then click and drag a border handle (□). To delete a user slice, click inside it and then press Del . When you resize or delete slices, Photoshop automatically resizes, creates, and deletes auto slices in the image to account for the change.

CHAPTER 5

Manipulating Selections

Making a selection defines a specific area of your Photoshop image. This chapter shows you how to move, stretch, erase, and manipulate your selections in a variety of ways.

Move a Selection

You can rearrange elements of your image by moving selections with the Move tool. This enables you to change the composition of your image to emphasize or de-emphasize certain elements. You can move elements of your image either in the default Background layer or in other layers you create for your image.

If you move elements in the Background layer, Photoshop fills the original location with the current background color. If you move elements in another layer, Photoshop makes the original location transparent, revealing any underlying layers. See Chapter 8 for more on layers.

Move a Selection

Move a Selected Object in the Background

1 Click the Background layer in the Layers panel.

If you start with a newly scanned image, Photoshop makes the Background layer the only layer.

2 Make a selection with a selection tool.

Note: See Chapter 4 for more on the selection tools. See Chapter 8 for more on layers.

3 Click the **Move** tool (⊹).

4 Click inside the selection and drag.

Ⓐ Photoshop fills the original location of the object with the current background color.

Ⓑ In this example, white is the background color.

Move a Selected Object in a Layer

1 Click a non-Background layer in the Layers panel.

2 Make a selection with a selection tool.

Note: See Chapter 4 for more on the selection tools. See Chapter 8 for more on layers.

3 Click the **Move** tool (⊹).

4 Click inside the selection and drag.

Photoshop moves the selection in the layer.

Photoshop fills the original location of the object with transparent pixels.

Note: Unlike the Background — Photoshop's opaque default layer — layers can include transparent pixels.

How do I move a selection in a straight line?

Press and hold Shift while you drag with the Move tool (⊹). Doing so constrains the movement of your object horizontally, vertically, or diagonally, depending on the direction you drag. You can also use the arrow keys to move a layer horizontally or vertically.

How do I move several layers at a time?

You can link the layers you want to move, select one of the linked layers, and then move them all with the Move tool (⊹). You can also Ctrl+click (⌘+click on a Mac) to select multiple layers and then move them with the Move tool. For more, see Chapter 8.

Copy and Paste a Selection

You can copy a selection and make a duplicate of it elsewhere in the image. You may use this technique to retouch an element in your photo by placing good content over bad. When you copy by using the Move tool and **Alt**, Photoshop keeps the duplicate in the same layer as the original.

You can also use the Copy and Paste commands to duplicate content in your image. This places the duplicate content in a new layer, which you can then move and transform independently. For more on using the Copy and Paste commands with layers, see Chapter 8.

Copy and Paste a Selection

Using the Keyboard and Mouse

1 Make a selection with a selection tool.

Note: See Chapter 4 for more on the selection tools.

2 Click the **Move** tool (![move]).

3 Press **Alt** (**Option** on a Mac) while you click and drag the object.

4 Release the mouse button to drop the selection.

Photoshop creates a duplicate of the object, which appears in the new location. The duplicate remains in the same layer as the original object.

Note: See Chapter 8 for more on layers.

Using the Copy and Paste Commands

1 Make a selection with a selection tool.

Note: See Chapter 4 for more on the selection tools.

2 Click **Edit**.

3 Click **Copy**.

4 Using a selection tool, select where you want to paste the copied element.

If you do not select an area, Photoshop pastes the copy over the original.

5 Click **Edit**.

6 Click **Paste**.

Ⓐ Photoshop pastes the copy into a new layer, which you can now move independently of the original image.

Note: See the section "Move a Selection" for more on moving your image.

How can I copy a selection from one window to another?
Click the **Move** tool (⯮) and then click and drag your selection from one window to another. If you are viewing multiple images in tabs, you can also drag your selection to another tab. You can also copy selections between windows by using the Copy and Paste commands in the Edit menu. To make multiple windows visible at the same time, see Chapter 2.

How can I copy content from multiple layers at once?
If your selection overlaps several layers in your image, you can click **Edit** and then **Copy Merged** to combine all the content into a single layer. Using the regular Copy command copies only from the selected layer. For more on layers, see Chapter 8.

Delete a Selection

Y ou can delete a selection to remove unwanted elements from an image. If you are working in the Background layer, you are given the choice of what color you want to fill the space with. If you are working in a layer other than the Background layer, deleting a selection turns the selected pixels transparent, and layers below it show through.

Another way to remove content from your image is to place that content in a layer and then hide the layer. You can reveal the layer to make the content reappear. For more about hiding layers, see Chapter 8.

Delete a Selection

1 Make a selection with a selection tool.

Note: See Chapter 4 for more on the selection tools.

Ⓐ In this example, a selection is deleted from the Background layer.

2 Press Del or Backspace.

The Fill window opens.

3 Click ▾ and select a fill option.

4 Click **OK**.

Ⓑ Photoshop deletes the selection.

In this example, Photoshop fills the deleted selection with the current background color.

If you delete pixels from a normal layer instead of the Background layer, Photoshop fills the selection with transparent pixels.

Rotate a Selection

You can rotate a selection to tilt an element or turn it upside down in your image. You may rotate an element to improve composition or to correct its appearance. The Free Rotate Selection command, located under the Rotate submenu, enables you to rotate a selection manually. Other rotate commands enable you to rotate a selection by degrees.

When you rotate a selection in the Background layer, Photoshop replaces the newly exposed areas with the background color. If you rotate a selection in another layer, the underlying layers appear in the exposed areas. See Chapter 8 for more on layers.

Rotate a Selection

1 Make a selection with a selection tool.

Note: See Chapter 4 for more on the selection tools.

2 Click **Edit**.

3 Click **Transform**.

4 Click **Rotate**.

A *bounding box*, a rectangular box with handles (☐) on the sides and corners, surrounds the object.

5 Click and drag to the side of the object.

The object rotates.

Note: You can rotate your selection precisely by typing percentage values in the W and H fields on the Options bar.

6 To apply the rotation, click ✔ or press Enter (⌘ + Return on a Mac).

Ⓐ To cancel, you can click ⊘ or press Esc.

Ⓑ In this example, a layer containing a Frisbee is rotated.

Note: See Chapter 8 for more on layers.

Scale a Selection

You can scale a selection to make it larger or smaller. Scaling enables you to adjust or emphasize parts of your image.

When you scale a selection smaller in the Background layer, Photoshop Elements replaces the newly exposed areas with the current background color. If you scale a selection in another layer, the underlying layers appear in the exposed areas. See Chapter 8 for more on layers. Scaling image content to a much larger size can decrease the quality of the content, making it blurry. You can correct blurriness using the Sharpen filter. See Chapter 10 for details.

Scale a Selection

1 Make a selection with a selection tool.

Note: See Chapter 4 for more on the selection tools.

2 Click **Edit**.

3 Click **Transform**.

4 Click **Scale**.

A rectangular bounding box with handles (☐) on the sides and corners surrounds the object.

5 Click and drag a corner handle (☐) to scale both the horizontal and vertical axes.

Note: You can scale your selection precisely by typing percentage values in the W and H fields on the Options bar.

6 Click and drag a side handle (□) to scale one axis at a time.

7 To apply the scaling, click ✔ or press Enter (⌘+Return on a Mac).

Ⓐ To cancel, you can click ⊘ or press Esc.

Photoshop scales the object to the new dimensions.

Ⓑ In this example, an object in the Background layer is scaled.

Note: See Chapter 8 for more on layers.

Ⓒ The area behind the object is filled with the background color.

How do I scale both dimensions proportionally?
You can press and hold Shift or click the **Maintain Aspect Ratio** icon (⬚) on the Options bar. When you scale your selection, the two axes of your selection grow or shrink proportionally; Photoshop does not distort your image.

How can I precisely double the size of my selection?
When scaling your selection, type **200%** in the W (width) and H (height) boxes on the Options bar. These boxes enable you to scale your selection to an exact percentage of its original size.

Skew or Distort a Selection

You can transform a selection by using the Skew or Distort commands. This enables you to stretch elements in your image into interesting shapes. You can also use skewing and distortion to change the perspective in your image, or make an object appear as if it recedes into the distance. When you skew or distort a selection in the Background layer, Photoshop replaces the newly exposed areas with the current background color. If you skew or distort a selection in another layer, the underlying layers appear in the exposed areas. See Chapter 8 for more on layers.

Skew or Distort a Selection

Skew a Selection

1 Make a selection with a selection tool.

Note: See Chapter 4 for more on the selection tools.

In this example, a flower in a layer is selected.

Note: See Chapter 8 for more about layers.

2 Click **Edit**.

3 Click **Transform**.

4 Click **Skew**.

Ⓐ A rectangular bounding box with handles (☐) on the sides and corners surrounds the object.

5 Click and drag a handle (☐) to skew the object.

Because the Skew command works along a single axis, you can drag either horizontally or vertically.

6 To apply the skewing, click ✔ or press Enter (⌘+Return on a Mac).

Ⓑ To cancel, you can click ⊘ or press Esc.

Distort a Selection

1 Make a selection with a selection tool.

Note: See Chapter 4 for more on the selection tools.

2 Click **Edit**.

3 Click **Transform**.

4 Click **Distort**.

ⓒ A rectangular bounding box with handles (☐) on the sides and corners surrounds the object.

5 Click and drag a handle (☐) to distort the object.

The Distort command works independently of the selection's different axes; you can drag a handle both vertically and horizontally.

Note: You can distort your selection precisely by typing percentage values or absolute values in the W and H fields on the Options bar.

6 To apply the distortion, click ☑ or press **Enter** (⌘+**Return** on a Mac).

ⓓ To cancel, you can click ⊘ or press **Esc**.

TIPS

How can I undo my skewing or distortion?
You can click **Edit** and then **Undo** to undo the last handle adjustment you made. This is an alternative to clicking ⊘, which cancels the entire Skew or Distort command.

How can I flip my image horizontally or vertically?
You can click **Edit**, **Transform**, and then **Flip Horizontal** or **Flip Vertical**. The Flip Horizontal command makes a selection look like its mirror image.

Perform Content-Aware Scaling

Y ou can use Photoshop's content-aware scaling feature to intelligently change the dimensions of an image. Important foreground objects stay the same size, but the less important background shrinks or enlarges.

This feature works best with landscape, beach, or water photos, where important objects stand out clearly from the rest of the scene. It works less well on more complex images. An alternative is to place objects you do not want to scale in a separate layer. For more about layers, see Chapter 8.

Perform Content-Aware Scaling

1 Click a layer to scale in the Layers panel.

Note: See Chapter 8 for more on layers.

2 Click **Select**.

3 Click **All**.

Photoshop selects all the pixels in your image.

4 Click **Edit**.

5 Click **Content-Aware Scale**.

Handles (□) appear on the edges of the selection.

6 Click and drag the handles (□) to shrink or enlarge the image.

In this example, the boy in the water remains unchanged, but the water surrounding him becomes smaller.

7 To apply the scaling, click ✓ or press **Enter** (⌘+**Return** on a Mac).

Ⓐ To cancel, you can click ⊘ or press **Esc**.

This shows the same example with the regular scale command applied. All the content in the image changes size equally.

Note: See the section "Scale a Selection" for more.

TIP

How can I improve content-aware scaling of images containing people?

You can use the Protect Skin Tones setting.

1 Follow steps **1** to **5** in this section to access content-aware scaling.

2 Click the **Protect Skin Tones** icon (🧍).

3 Click and drag the handles (□) to scale the image.

Objects in the image with skin tones are protected.

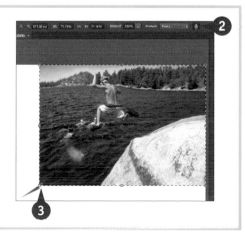

Refine a Selection Edge

You can open the Refine Edge dialog box to make a variety of adjustments to the edge of your selection. For example, you can shift the edge in or out or smooth any sharp angles along an edge.

For more on feathering an edge by using the Refine Edge dialog box, see the section "Feather the Border of a Selection."

Refine a Selection Edge

1 Make a selection with a selection tool.

Note: See Chapter 4 for more on the selection tools.

When a selection tool is active, Photoshop displays a Refine Edge button.

2 Click **Refine Edge**.

The Refine Edge dialog box opens.

Photoshop displays the selected element to make the selection more apparent.

3 Click and drag the **Radius** slider (◨) to the right to expand the area considered for automatic selection.

Photoshop examines the color transitions near the edge and adjusts the selection to account for them.

4 Click and drag the **Smooth** slider (⬜) to the right to smooth sharp angles along the edge.

Smoothing can be useful after selecting with the Polygonal Lasso, which can create a selection with sharp points.

5 Click and drag the **Shift Edge** slider (⬜) to move the edge in or out from the selected object.

Drag to the left to move the edge in.

Drag to the right to move the edge out.

6 Click **OK**.

Photoshop adjusts the selection.

TIP

How do I improve selections along hair and other complex elements?

1 Complete steps **1** and **2** in this section.

2 Click and drag the **Radius** slider (⬜) to the right to expand the area considered by the selection tool.

3 Click the **Decontaminate Colors** check box (⬜ changes to ☑).

4 Click **OK**.

Ⓐ Photoshop adjusts the edge.

Feather the Border of a Selection

You can feather a selection's border to create soft edges. Feathering enables you to control the sharpness of the edges in a selection. You can use this technique with other layers to create a blending effect between the selected area and any underlying layers. Soft edges around content can add a sentimental or romantic feel to your image.

To create a soft edge around an object, you must first select the object, feather the selection border, and then delete the part of the image that surrounds your selection. You can change the final effect achieved by changing the applied background color.

Feather the Border of a Selection

Select and Feather the Image

1 Make a selection with a selection tool.

Note: See Chapter 4 for more on the selection tools.

When a selection tool is active, Photoshop displays a Refine Edge button.

2 Click **Refine Edge**.

The Refine Edge dialog box opens.

3 Type a pixel value between 0.1 and 250 in the Feather text field to determine the softness of the edge.

The larger the number, the thicker the softened edge.

4 Click **OK**.

Delete the Surrounding Background

1 Click **Select**.

2 Click **Inverse**.

The selection inverts but remains feathered.

3 Press Del.

The Fill window opens.

4 Click ☐ and select a fill color.

5 Click **OK**.

Photoshop fills the selection and applies the feathering to the image.

What happens if I feather a selection and then apply a command to it?
Photoshop applies the command only partially to pixels near the edge of the selection. For example, if you remove color from a selection by using the Hue/Saturation command, color at the feathered edge of the selection is only partially removed. For more on the Hue/Saturation command, see Chapter 7.

Is there another way to feather my selection?
When selecting with the Marquee or Lasso tool, you can create a feathered selection by first typing a pixel value greater than 0 in the Feather text field on the Options bar. Your resulting selection will have a feathered edge.

Create Vanishing Point Planes

Y ou can model the 3-D characteristics of flat objects in your image by creating planes with the Vanishing Point tool. This can be useful if you work with objects such as the sides of buildings, interior walls, or table surfaces. To create a vanishing point plane, you specify the corners of a flat surface in your image. You can create multiple planes in a single image.

After you create vanishing point planes, you can apply special Photoshop commands. See the section "Copy between Vanishing Point Planes" for more.

Create Vanishing Point Planes

1 Open an image that includes flat surfaces.

Note: See Chapter 1 for more on opening an image.

2 Click **Filter**.

3 Click **Vanishing Point**.

The Vanishing Point dialog box opens.

4 Click the **Create Plane** tool (▦).

5 Click to mark a corner of a plane.

6 Click a second time to mark another corner.

Photoshop connects the points to create a plane edge.

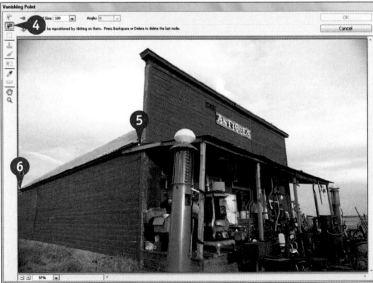

7 Click two more times to mark the final two corners of the plane.

Photoshop creates the vanishing point plane.

A You can use the Edit Plane tool (⌖) to move a plane or adjust its corners or sides.

8 Click ⌖ again.

9 Click four more times to create another vanishing point plane.

Photoshop creates the vanishing point plane, which is oriented differently from the first.

To delete a plane, select it with ⌖ and then press Del.

10 Click **OK**.

Photoshop saves your work and closes the dialog box.

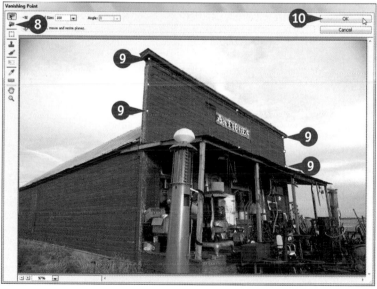

Why is it called the Vanishing Point tool?
In perspective drawing, the vanishing point is the point on the horizon where receding parallel lines appear to meet. Photoshop uses such parallel lines to represent the planes in the Vanishing Point dialog box.

How can I add perspective to objects in my image?
You can resize objects in your image to make them appear to recede into the distance with the Perspective command. After you select an object, click **Edit**, **Transform**, and then **Perspective**. The command works similarly to the Distort and Skew commands. See "Skew or Distort a Selection" for details.

Copy between Vanishing Point Planes

After you define one or more vanishing point planes in an image, you can edit and transform objects within the planes. For example, you can copy an object between two vanishing point planes. Photoshop transforms the object as you move it so it conforms to the orientation of the current plane.

To define planes in an image, see "Create Vanishing Point Panes."

Copy between Vanishing Point Planes

① Create vanishing point planes in your image.

Note: For more, see the section "Create Vanishing Point Planes."

② Click **Filter**.

③ Click **Vanishing Point**.

The Vanishing Point dialog box opens, displaying the different planes.

④ Click the **Rectangular Marquee** tool (▦).

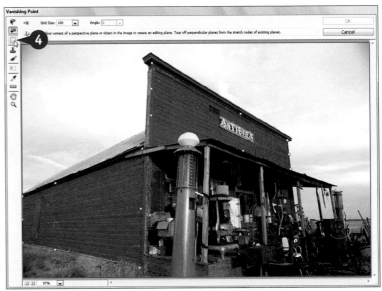

⑤ Click and drag to select an object inside a plane.

Photoshop draws a marquee whose sides are parallel to those of the plane.

6 Press and hold Alt (Option on a Mac).

7 Click and drag the selection from one plane to another.

Photoshop transforms the selection to orient it with the destination plane.

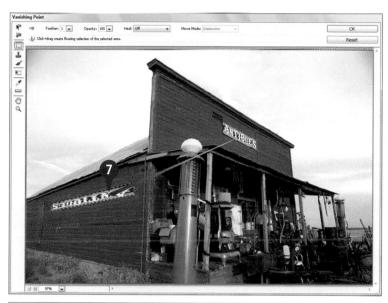

8 Click the **Transform** tool (⬚).

9 Click the **Flip** check box (☐ changes to ☑) to flip the selection horizontally.

10 Click the **Flop** check box (☐ changes to ☑) to flip the selection vertically.

11 Click **OK**.

Photoshop saves your work and closes the dialog box.

TIPS

What does the Brush tool (✏) do in the Vanishing Point dialog box?

Like the normal Brush tool, it applies the foreground color to objects in your image. But in the Vanishing Point dialog box, the brush shape conforms to the plane in which you paint. You can control the characteristics of the brush with the settings at the top of the dialog box.

What does the Stamp tool (🖳) do in the Vanishing Point dialog box?

It enables you to clone content from one Vanishing Point plane to another. The cloned pixels conform to the shape of the current plane.

Using the Content-Aware Move Tool

You can move an object in your image and have Photoshop automatically fill in the space where the object was originally with surrounding content. Photoshop takes into account the colors and textures around the object when filling in the original location. This is in contrast to using the Move tool, which fills the original space with the current Background color or transparent pixels. See "Move a Selection" for details. For best results with the Content-Aware Move tool, select an object in an area of continuous color and texture. The Content-Aware Move tool is new in Photoshop CS6.

Using the Content-Aware Move Tool

1 Click and hold the **Spot Healing Brush** tool (🖊).

2 In the list that appears, click the **Content-Aware Move** tool (✄).

A Make sure the Mode is set to Move.

3 Click and drag to select the object you want to move.

Note: The tool works similarly to the Lasso tool. See Chapter 4 for details.

Alternatively, you can first select with a different selection tool and then select the Content-Aware Move tool.

④ Click inside the selection and drag to another location in your image.

⑤ Release the mouse button.

🅑 Photoshop copies the object to the new location.

🅒 The original location is filled with surrounding content.

TIP

How can I extend an object in my image?
You can use the Content-Aware Move tool to extend objects such as buildings and fences.

① With the Content-Aware Move tool (🔀) selected, click ▤ and select **Extend**.

② Select an object.

③ Click and drag the selection.

④ Release the mouse button.

Photoshop extends the object, making color and texture adjustments based on the content near the selection.

105

CHAPTER 6

Painting and Drawing with Color

You can add splashes, streaks, or solid areas of color to your image. Photoshop offers a variety of tools with which you can add almost any color or texture imaginable. This chapter introduces you to those tools and shows you how to choose your colors.

Select the Foreground and Background Colors

You can select colors to use with many of the painting and drawing tools in Photoshop by setting the foreground and background colors. The Brush and Pencil tools apply the foreground color, and the Eraser tool applies the background color when used on the Background layer. See the section "Using the Brush Tool" for more on how to paint on a photo. See the section "Using the Eraser" for more on using the Eraser.

Some filters in Photoshop apply their effects to your image based on the current foreground and background colors. See Chapter 10 for more about filters.

Select the Foreground and Background Colors

Select the Foreground Color

1 Click the **Foreground Color** box.

The Color Picker dialog box opens.

Ⓐ To change the range of colors that appears in the color box, click and drag the slider (⬚).

2 Click the color you want as the foreground color in the color box.

3 Click **OK**.

Ⓑ The selected color appears in the Foreground Color box.

4 Click a painting tool in the Toolbox.

This example uses the Brush tool (🖌).

Note: For more on painting tools, see the section "Using the Brush Tool."

5 Click and drag to apply the color.

Select the Background Color

1 Click the **Background Color** box.

The Color Picker dialog box opens.

C To change the range of colors that appears in the color box, click and drag the slider ($\triangleright\boxed{}\triangleleft$).

2 To select a background color, click the color you want in the color box.

3 Click **OK**.

D The selected color appears in the Background Color box.

4 Click the **Eraser** tool (▨).

5 Click and drag the cursor (◯).

The tool erases by painting with the background color.

Note: Painting occurs only when erasing in the Background layer; in other layers, the eraser turns pixels transparent. See Chapter 8 for a full discussion of layers.

TIPS

How do I reset the foreground and background colors?

Click the **Default** icon (▣) to the lower left of the Foreground and Background icons. Doing so resets the colors to black and white.

What is a web-safe color?

Web browsers on some older monitors can display only colors from a specific 216-color palette. These colors are known as web-safe colors. You can click the **Only Web Colors** check box in the Color Picker dialog box (▣ changes to ☑) to restrict your choices to web-safe colors.

Select a Color with the Eyedropper Tool

You can select a color from an open image with the Eyedropper tool. The Eyedropper tool enables you to paint by using a color already present in your image. You place the tool over a color in your image and click to load that color as your foreground or background color. For more about setting colors, see "Select the Foreground and Background Colors."

Settings in the Options bar enable you to customize the area of the image from which you are sampling.

Select a Color with the Eyedropper Tool

1 Click the **Eyedropper** tool (🖌).

2 Position 🖉 over your image.

You can click **Window** and then **Info** to open the Info panel to see color values as you move 🖉.

3 Click to select the color of the pixel beneath the tip of 🖉.

A The color becomes the new foreground color.

To select a new background color, you can press **Alt** (**Option** on a Mac) as you click in step **3**.

You can temporarily employ the Eyedropper tool when using a painting tool, such as the Brush or Paint Bucket, by pressing and holding **Alt** (**Option** on a Mac).

Select a Color with the Swatches Panel

You can select a color with the Swatches panel. The Swatches panel enables you to choose from a small set of commonly used colors. You place the tool over a color in the panel and click to load that color as your foreground or background color. For more about setting colors, see "Select the Foreground and Background Colors."

You can also add colors to the Swatches panel using the Eyedropper tool. This is useful for saving colors you might want to use later.

Select a Color with the Swatches Panel

1 Click **Window**.

2 Click **Swatches**.

3 Position your cursor over a color swatch.

   changes to .

4 Click a color swatch to select a foreground color.

A The color becomes the new foreground color.

To select a background color, press Alt (Option on a Mac) as you click in step **4**.

You can use the Eyedropper tool ( ) to add the current foreground color to the Swatches panel. After selecting the tool, position it over the empty area of the panel and then click.

Using the Brush Tool

You can use the Brush tool to add patches of solid color to your image. You can use the tool to cover unwanted elements or change the appearance of clothing or a backdrop. When applying the Brush tool, you can control the size of the brushstrokes by choosing a brush size. For realistic results, turn on the Airbrush feature to apply a softer line of color.

To limit where the brush applies color, create a selection before using the tool. For more, see Chapter 4. To customize the brush to apply different patterns of color, see "Change Brush Styles."

Using the Brush Tool

1 Click the **Brush** tool (▨).

2 Click the **Foreground Color** box to select a color with which to paint.

Note: For more, see the section "Select the Foreground and Background Colors."

3 Click here (▤) to open the Brush menu to choose a brush size and type.

Note: To access different brush styles, see the section "Change Brush Styles."

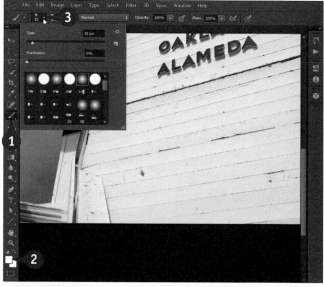

4 Click and drag to apply the foreground color to the image.

To undo the most recent brush stroke, you can click **Edit** and then **Undo Brush**.

Note: To undo more than one brush stroke using the History panel, see Chapter 2.

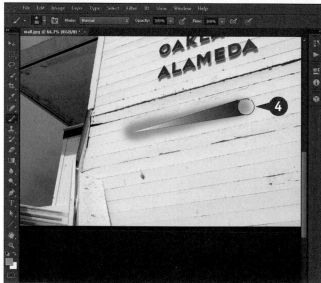

5 Type a percentage value to change the opacity of the brush strokes.

Ⓐ Alternatively, you can click here (▪) to adjust the Opacity slider.

6 Click and drag to apply the semitransparent paintbrush.

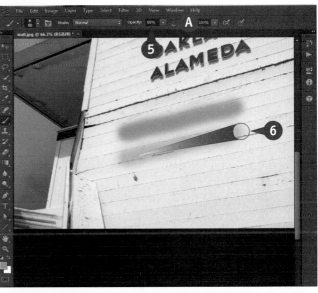

7 Type a percentage value to change how much color the brush applies.

Ⓑ Alternatively, you can click here (▪) to adjust the Flow slider.

8 Click and drag to apply the customized brush.

Photoshop applies color per your specifications.

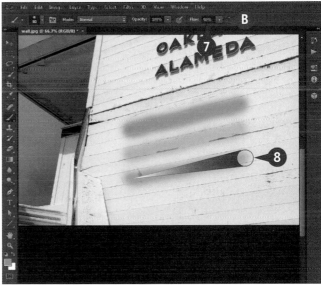

TIPS

What are the Pencil and Airbrush tools?
You can use the Pencil tool to draw hard-edged lines of color. To access the Pencil tool, click and hold the **Brush** tool (🖌) and then click 🖉. The Airbrush tool paints soft lines that get darker the longer you hold down your mouse button. You can convert your brush to an airbrush by clicking the **Airbrush** button (🖌) on the Options bar.

What is a virtual slider?
You can adjust certain slider-based settings, such as the Opacity and Fill settings in the Layers panel, by positioning the cursor over the setting's label and clicking and dragging. For example, you can position your mouse pointer over **Opacity** and then click and drag to the left or right to decrease or increase the currently selected layer's opacity.

Change Brush Styles

You can select from a variety of predefined brush styles in Photoshop to apply color to your image in different ways. Brush styles can have hard or soft edges. Brush styles with specialized tips can apply speckled patterns of color to your image. Photoshop offers a variety of predefined brush sets that you can access in the Options bar.

Change Brush Styles

① Click the **Brush** tool (✍).

② Click here (▾) to open the Brush menu.

③ Click ⚙.

The Brush menu opens.

④ Click a set of brushes.

A dialog box opens, asking if you want to replace your brushes.

⑤ Click **OK**.

Ⓐ To add the set of brushes to the currently displayed set, click **Append**.

If a dialog box opens asking if you want to save the current brush set, click **No**.

Note: You can reset your brushes to the original set by choosing **Reset Brushes** from the Brush menu.

The new set appears in the Brush list.

6 Click a brush style.

7 Click here to set the foreground and background colors for the brush.

Note: See "Select the Foreground and Background Colors" for details.

8 Click and drag to apply the new brush.

Photoshop applies color with the brush.

TIP

What are bristle-tip brushes?
With bristle-tip brushes, Photoshop models the behavior of real-world bristles to allow for lifelike strokes.

1 Click **Window** and then **Brush**. The Brush panel opens.

2 In the Brush panel, click a bristle-tip brush.

3 Specify the bristle settings for the brush.

A Photoshop displays the type of stroke that the brush applies.

Create a Custom Brush

You can use the Brushes panel to create one-of-a-kind brushes of varying sizes and shapes. For example, you can adjust the roundness and angle of a brush tip to create a slanted brush, or decrease the hardness to make a brush apply softer textures. You can even specify a brush shape that changes as it paints, enabling you to generate a random design.

After you design your new brush, you can save it in the Brush menu so you can quickly access it in the future.

Create a Custom Brush

1 Click the **Brush** tool (✐).

2 Click **Window**.

3 Click **Brushes**.

The Brush panel opens.

4 Click **Brush Tip Shape**.

5 Click a brush style to use as a starting point for your custom brush.

6 Click and drag the **Size** slider (🖌) to change the brush size.

7 Type a Roundness value between 0% and 100%.

The lower the number, the more oval the brush.

You can adjust other settings to further define the tip shape.

8 Click the **Shape Dynamics** check box (☐ changes to ☑).

9 Click and drag the **Size Jitter** slider (📷) to specify the amount your brush varies in size as it paints.

10 Click and drag the **Minimum Diameter** slider (📷) to specify the smallest size to which the brush scales when Size Jitter is enabled.

11 Click and drag the other sliders (📷) to control how the brush angle and roundness change.

You can click other categories to define other settings.

12 Click ✕ to close the Brush panel.

13 Click and drag inside the image.

Photoshop applies the custom brush.

TIP

How do I save my custom brush in the Brush drop-down menu?

1 In the Brush panel, click 📑.

2 Click **New Brush Preset**.

The Brush Name dialog box opens.

3 Type a name in the Brush Name dialog box.

4 Click **OK**.

Photoshop adds your brush to the Brush menu.

Using the Mixer Brush

The Mixer Brush mixes colors that you paint, just as wet paint mixes on a real canvas. The tool enables you to produce effects similar to those you can get by using real watercolors and oils.

You specify what color the brush should apply as well as how much is deposited as you paint. You also specify a wetness setting that determines how much the existing color in the image is affected as you click and drag the tool. The Mixer Brush debuted in Photoshop CS5.

Using the Mixer Brush

1. Click and hold the **Brush** tool (▨).

2. In the list that appears, click the **Mixer Brush** tool (▨).

3. Click here (▾) to choose a brush size.

4. Click here to choose a color with which to paint.

5. Click here (▾) to specify a **Wet** setting.

   This controls how much color from the image the brush picks up.

6. Click here (▾) to specify a **Load** setting.

   This controls how much color is loaded on the brush prior to applying the brush.

7. Click here (▾) to specify a **Flow** setting.

   This controls the rate at which the brush deposits color on the image.

A. You can select from several presets to combine different brush settings.

8. Click and drag to apply the color.

B Photoshop applies the color, mixing it with the colors already in the image.

9 Click here to choose a different color to apply.

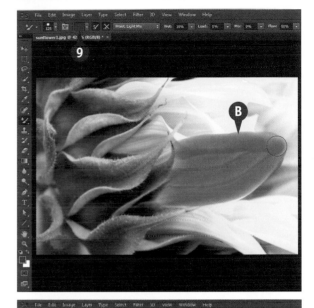

10 Click and drag to apply the color to the image.

C Photoshop applies the second color.

The second color is mixed with the first where the colors cross.

TIP

What are the different brush settings for the Mixer Brush?

The Current Brush Load menu enables you to load the brush with the selected color or clean the brush, which removes the loaded color. Applying a clean brush mixes existing colors in the image without applying new color.

Selecting Load Brush (▨) adds color to the brush after each stroke. When the option is deselected, the brush dries out over successive strokes.

Selecting Clean Brush (▨) removes any color on the brush after each stroke. When the option is deselected, color picked up from the image is applied over successive strokes.

Apply a Gradient

You can apply a *gradient*, which is a blend from one color to another, to give objects in your image a radiant or 3-D look. You can apply a gradient to a selected portion of an image or the entire image. Setting the geometry of a gradient controls the direction of the color blend. A linear gradient changes as it moves across your image. A radial gradient changes color from a center point moving outward.

The Gradient Editor enables you to choose from predefined color combinations for your gradient or choose your own custom colors.

Apply a Gradient

1 Make a selection.

In this example, the entire background layer is selected.

Note: See Chapter 4 for more on making selections.

2 Click the **Gradient** tool (▣).

A A linear gradient is the default. This creates a gradient straight across your selection. You can select different geometries on the Options bar.

3 Click the gradient swatch.

The Gradient Editor opens.

4 Select a gradient type from the Presets area.

B Photoshop shows the settings for the selected gradient below.

You can customize the gradient by changing the settings.

5 Click **OK**.

6 Click and drag inside the selection.

The direction and transition of the gradient are defined.

Note: Dragging a long line with the tool produces a gradual transition; dragging a short line produces an abrupt transition.

C Photoshop generates a gradient inside the selection.

TIP

How can I customize the colors and opacity of my gradient?
Use the controls at the bottom of the Gradient Editor.

A Click the color stops to define the colors in a gradient.

B Click the opacity stops to define the transparency of the gradient colors.

C You can click and drag the midpoint icon to specify where the gradient's transition occurs.

Fill a Selection

You can fill a selection with a solid color by using the Fill command. This enables you to change the color of a selected object or quickly paint over a large area. You can customize your fill by changing the opacity and mode. This can enable you to add color to your image and still let the texture of the original image show through the new fill color.

Fill a Selection

1 Define the area you want to fill by using a selection tool.

Note: See Chapter 4 for more on the selection tools.

2 Click **Edit**.

3 Click **Fill**.

The Fill dialog box opens.

4 Click here (⊡) to choose a fill option.

Ⓐ You can also fill your selection with a custom pattern. For more on using this option, see the tip in the section "Using the Pattern Stamp."

To fill the selection with other content from the scene, see the section "Using Content-Aware Fill."

Ⓑ You can decrease the opacity to fill with a semitransparent color or pattern.

5 Click **OK**.

C Photoshop fills the area.

D You can select other areas and then fill them with different colors.

This example uses a fill with the mode set to Color.

Note: For more on blending modes, see Chapter 8.

How do I apply a "ghosted" white covering over part of an image?
Use a selection tool to define the area of the image that you want to cover and then apply the Fill command with white selected and the opacity set to less than 50%.

How can I quickly fill similarly colored areas with a new color?
You can use the Paint Bucket tool (🪣) to fill contiguous areas in your image with the current color. You can set the Paint Bucket's tolerance value to determine the range of colors the paint bucket affects when you apply it. A low tolerance value affects a narrow range of colors, whereas a high tolerance value affects a wide range.

Using Content-Aware Fill

You can use the Content-Aware setting, which is new in Photoshop CS6, with the Fill command to automatically analyze the makeup of your image and intelligently fill the selection with other content in the scene.

Using Content-Aware Fill

1 Define the area you want to fill by using a selection tool.

Note: See Chapter 4 for more on the selection tools.

In this example, the baseball player is selected.

2 Click **Edit**.

3 Click **Fill**.

The Fill dialog box opens.

4 Click here ( ) to choose **Content-Aware**.

5 Click **OK**.

A Photoshop fills the area with surrounding content.

6 Click the **Clone Stamp** tool (![icon]).

7 You can optionally apply the Clone Stamp tool to fix areas of the fill.

Note: For more on the Clone Stamp tool, see the section "Using the Clone Stamp."

TIP

How do I apply a content-aware fill with the Spot Healing Brush tool?

1 Click the **Spot Healing Brush** tool (![icon]).

2 Click the **Content-Aware** radio button (![icon] changes to ![icon]).

3 Click and drag over the object you want to replace.

Photoshop replaces the object with other content in the image.

Stroke a Selection

You can use the Stroke command to draw a line along the edge of a selection. This can help you highlight objects in your image or add decoration to text. When you apply a stroke, you specify its color, width, and location. The location can be the inside, outside, or center of the selection. You can apply a semitransparent line to an object by decreasing the opacity of the stroke.

A stroke may also be applied as a layer style. For more about layer styles, see Chapter 9.

Stroke a Selection

1. Select an area of the image with a selection tool.

Note: See Chapter 4 for more on the selection tools.

2. Click **Edit**.

3. Click **Stroke**.

The Stroke dialog box opens.

4. Type a width in pixels.

5. Click the **Inside** radio button to stroke a line on the inside of the selection, the **Center** radio button to stroke a line straddling the selection, or the **Outside** radio button to stroke a line on the outside of the selection (⊙ changes to ⊙).

Ⓐ You can click the **Color** box to define the color of the stroke.

6. Click **OK**.

B Photoshop strokes a line along the selection.

You can select other areas and stroke them by using different settings.

C This stroke was applied to the inside of the selection at 50% opacity.

TIPS

How do I add a colored border to my image?
Click **Select** and then **All**. Apply the Stroke command, clicking the **Inside** radio button as the location (⊙ changes to ⊙). Photoshop adds a border to the image.

How do I stroke a line a fixed distance outside of an object?
After selecting the object, you can expand your selection and then stroke the line. To expand a selection, click **Select**, **Modify**, and then **Expand**. For more on making selections, see Chapter 4.

Using the Clone Stamp

You can clean up small flaws or erase elements in your image with the Clone Stamp tool. The tool copies information from one area of an image to another. For example, you can use the Clone Stamp tool to remove unwanted blemishes of all kinds by cloning an area near the flaw and then stamping over the flaw.

You can adjust the opacity of the tool to copy information partially to the new location. Lowering the opacity and then copying from multiple areas in an image can sometimes be the best way to cleanly erase an unwanted object.

Using the Clone Stamp

1 Click the **Clone Stamp** tool (🔲).

2 Click here (🔽) to open the Brush menu to choose a brush size and type.

3 Press and hold Alt (Option on a Mac) and then click the area of the image from which you want to copy.

A You can specify an opacity of less than 100% to partially apply the tool.

You do not need to select an area inside the current image; you can Alt+click (Option+click on a Mac) another open image.

This example uses the tool to select an area of water in the pond.

4 Release **Alt** (**Option** on a Mac).

5 Click and drag to apply the Clone Stamp.

Photoshop copies the previously clicked area to where you click and drag.

B As you apply the tool, a preview of the content to be cloned appears inside the brush cursor (○).

C A + appears at the location from which you are cloning.

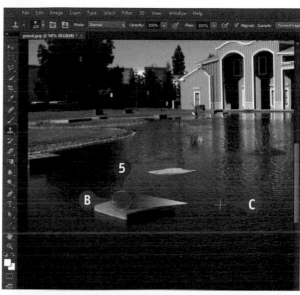

6 Click and drag repeatedly over the image to achieve the desired effect.

As you apply the tool, you can press **Alt** (**Option** on a Mac) and then click again to select a different area from which to copy.

TIP

How can I make the Clone Stamp's effects look seamless?
To erase elements from your image with the Clone Stamp without leaving a trace, try the following:

Clone between areas of similar color and texture.

To apply the Clone Stamp more subtly, lower its opacity on the Options bar.

After you click 🔽 to open the Brush menu, choose a soft-edged brush shape.

Using the Pattern Stamp

You can paint with a pattern by using the Pattern Stamp tool. This tool gives you a free-form way to add repeating elements to your images. You paint patterns onto your image by clicking and dragging with the tool.

Photoshop comes with a few basic patterns, but you can create more from your own images. You can select a rectangular area of your image and then set the area as a pattern with the Define Pattern command. The area will then show up in the Pattern menu for the tool to use.

Using the Pattern Stamp

Select a Pattern

① Click and hold the **Clone Stamp** tool (⬛).

② In the list that appears, click the **Pattern Stamp** tool (⬛).

③ Click here (▣) to open the Brush menu to choose a brush size and type.

④ Click here (▣) to open the Pattern menu.

⑤ Select a pattern to apply.

Ⓐ You can click the **Aligned** check box (⬛ changes to ☑) to make your strokes paint the pattern as contiguous tiles.

To create a custom pattern, see the tip at the end of this section.

6 Click and drag to apply the pattern.

Photoshop applies the pattern wherever you click and drag.

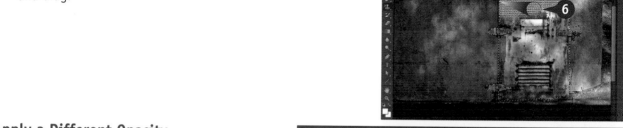

Apply a Different Opacity

1 Type a value of less than 100% in the Opacity box.

2 Click and drag inside the selection to apply the pattern.

Decreasing the opacity causes the brush to apply a semitransparent pattern.

TIP

How do I define my own custom patterns?

1 Click the **Rectangular Marquee** tool (▦).

2 Select an area in your image to use as a pattern.

3 Click **Edit** and then **Define Pattern** to open the Pattern Name dialog box.

A Your pattern appears in the preview in the dialog box.

4 In the Pattern Name dialog box, type a name for your pattern.

5 Click **OK**.

Using the Spot Healing Brush

You can heal imperfections in your image with the Spot Healing Brush tool. You click and drag over an object in your image with the brush, and Photoshop intelligently copies nearby pixels to remove the object. The tool works best if the object in your image is in an area with consistent and continuous color and texture.

The Spot Healing Brush is a less interactive version of the Healing Brush. You can try the Healing Brush instead if your results with the Spot Healing Brush are less than optimal. See "Using the Healing Brush" for details.

Using the Spot Healing Brush

1. Click the **Spot Healing Brush** tool (🖌).

2. Click here (▾) to open the Brush menu.

3. Specify a brush size.

   If the area you want to heal is small, choose a brush size that covers the area.

4. You can click and drag ■ to adjust the shape of the brush.

5 Click the area you want to heal.

Photoshop shades the area.

You can click and drag to paint over a large area.

A Photoshop automatically heals the selected area. It replaces the imperfection inside the selected area with the surrounding colors and textures.

TIPS

What type setting should I use for the Spot Healing Brush?
You can click a type setting (⊙ changes to ⊙) in the Options bar to control how Photoshop heals the area of your image. Content-Aware is typically the best setting because it takes into account the edges and shadows around the selected area. Proximity Match uses the pixels adjacent to the edge of the selection, whereas Create Texture uses pixels within the selection.

How can I reset a tool to its default settings?
Right-click (Ctrl+click on a Mac) the tool's icon on the far left side of the Options bar and then click **Reset Tool** from the menu that appears.

Using the Healing Brush

You can correct defects in your image by using the Healing Brush. The Healing Brush is similar to the Clone Stamp in that it copies pixels from one area of the image to another. However, the Healing Brush takes into account the texture and lighting of the image as it works, which can make its modifications more convincing.

Another option is the Spot Healing Brush, which automatically heals the area of your image that you paint over. See "Using the Spot Healing Brush" for more details.

Using the Healing Brush

1 Click and hold the **Spot Healing Brush** tool (🖌).

2 In the list that appears, click the **Healing Brush** tool (🖌).

3 Click here (▾) to open the Brush menu to specify your brush settings.

A Make sure to click the **Sampled** radio button (◉ changes to ◉).

4 Press and hold Alt (Option on a Mac) and then click the source area of the image you want to heal with.

5 Release **Alt** (**Option** on a Mac).

6 Click and drag inside the selection to apply the Healing Brush.

Photoshop copies the selected area wherever you click and drag.

7 Stop dragging and then release the mouse button.

Photoshop adjusts the copied pixels to account for the lighting and texture present in the image.

TIP

How can I more easily work from several different source images?

1 With the Healing Brush selected, click ▣ in the Options bar.

The Clone Source panel opens. As you define source areas from your images, Photoshop makes them accessible here.

2 Click ▣ to clone from a source area.

Ⓐ You can click here to turn the cursor overlay off (☑ changes to ▢).

Using the Patch Tool

The Patch tool enables you to correct defects in your image by selecting them and then dragging the selection to an unflawed area of the image. This can be useful if a large part of your image is free of flaws such as with a clear blue sky, lawn, or blank wall.

For other ways to correct defects in your image, see the sections "Using Content-Aware Fill," "Using the Clone Stamp," "Using the Spot Healing Brush," and "Using the Healing Brush."

Using the Patch Tool

1 Click and hold the **Spot Healing Brush** tool (◢).

2 In the list that appears, click the **Patch** tool (▦).

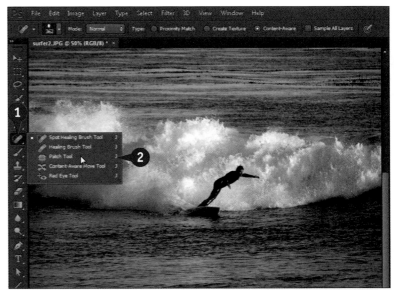

3 Click and drag to select the part of your image that contains the defects you want to patch.

When you make selections, the Patch tool works similar to the Lasso tool.

Note: See Chapter 4 for more on the Lasso tool.

4 Click inside the selection and then drag it to an area that does not have defects.

A Photoshop uses pixels from the destination selection to patch the defects in the source selection.

B You can click the Destination radio button (⊙ changes to ⦿) to patch defects in the reverse order; flaws in the destination selection are corrected with the pixels from the source selection.

TIPS

How does the Patch tool determine what are defects in my selection?

It does this by comparing the colors and textures in the two selections. The tool then tries to eliminate the differences — the defects — while retaining the overall color and texture.

Can I use other selection tools to create my patch selection?

Yes. You can use selection tools, such as the Marquee tools and the Lasso tools, to define the area you want to patch. Then, you can use the Patch tool (▦) to click and drag the selection to complete the patch.

Using the History Brush

You can use the History Brush tool to paint a previous state of your image from the History panel into the current image. This can be useful if you want to revert just a part of your image. You specify the image version that you want to copy from by defining a snapshot in the History panel. For example, you can define as a snapshot a version of your image before any filters were applied, and then paint parts of that version back onto the finished image. For more about the History panel, see the "Undo Commands" section in Chapter 2.

Using the History Brush

Paint a Previous State

1 Click **Window**.

2 Click **History**.

The History panel opens.

3 Click the **Create New Snapshot** button (🔲) in the History panel.

A Photoshop puts a copy of the current state of the image into the History panel.

4 Modify your image to make it different from the newly created snapshot.

In this example, the Solarize and Watercolor filters were applied.

5 Click to the left of the snapshot to select it as the History brush source.

6 Click the **History Brush** tool (⬛).

7 Click here (⬛) to open the Brush menu to specify your brush settings.

8 Click and drag inside the image.

Pixels from the previous snapshot are painted into the image.

Using the Art History Brush

1 Click and hold the **History Brush** tool (⬛).

2 In the list that appears, click the **Art History Brush** tool (⬛).

With the Art History Brush tool, you can paint-in snapshot information with an added impressionistic effect.

3 Click here (⬛) to open the Brush menu to specify your brush settings.

4 Click and drag to apply an artistic effect.

TIP

How do I paint onto a blank image with the History Brush tool?
Start with a photographic image, take a snapshot of it with the **Create New Snapshot** button (⬛), and then fill the image with a solid color. See the section "Fill a Selection" for more. You can then use the History Brush tool (⬛) to paint-in the photographic content.

Using the Eraser

You can use the Eraser tool to erase unwanted areas of your photo. When you apply the Eraser tool in the Background layer, the erased pixels are replaced with the current background color. When you erase in other layers, the Eraser tool turns the pixels transparent, revealing any underlying layers.

In the Options bar, you can control the size of the eraser and the softness of its edges. Using a soft-edged eraser can be useful for removing content around objects that have fuzzy edges. You can also change the opacity of the tool to only partially erase content in your image.

Using the Eraser

In the Background Layer

1 Click the Background layer in the Layers panel.

If you start with a newly scanned image, the Background layer is the only layer.

Note: See Chapter 8 for more on layers.

2 Click the **Eraser** tool ().

3 Click here () to open the Brush menu to choose a brush size and type.

4 Click and drag inside the image.

A Photoshop erases the image by painting with the background color.

In a Regular Layer

1 Click a layer other than the Background layer in the Layers panel.

Note: See Chapter 8 for more on layers.

2 Click the **Eraser** tool (🖫).

3 Click here (🔽) to open the **Brush** menu to choose a brush size and type.

4 Click and drag inside the image.

Photoshop erases elements in the layer by making pixels transparent.

TIP

How can I quickly erase areas of similar color in my image?
If you click and hold the **Eraser** tool (🖫) in the Toolbox, a list appears, and you can select the **Background Eraser** (🖫) or the **Magic Eraser** (🖫). The Background Eraser works by sampling the pixel color beneath the center of the brush and erasing similar colors that are underneath the brush. The Magic Eraser also samples the color beneath the cursor but erases similar pixels throughout the layer. You can adjust the tolerance of both tools on the Options bar to control how much they erase.

Replace a Color

You can replace colors in your image with the current foreground color by using the Color Replacement tool. This gives you a free-form way of recoloring objects in your image while keeping the shading on the objects intact.

Replace a Color

1 Click and hold the **Brush** tool ( ).

2 In the list that appears, click the **Color Replacement** tool ( ).

3 Click the **Foreground Color** box to select a color for painting.

Note: For more, see the section "Select the Foreground and Background Colors."

4 Click here ( ) to open the Brush menu to choose a brush size and type.

5 Click the **Sampling: Continuous** icon ( ).

Sampling: Continuous samples different colors to replace as you paint.

A Sampling: Once ( ) samples only the first color you click.

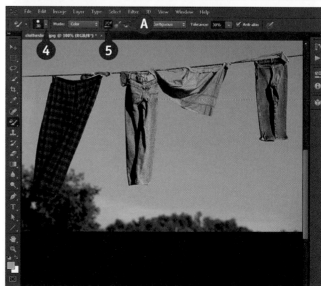

6 Type a tolerance from 1% to 100%.

The greater the tolerance, the greater the range of colors the tool replaces.

7 Click and drag in your image to replace color.

8 Continue to click and drag in your image.

Photoshop replaces more color.

How does the Color Replacement tool decide what colors to replace?
When you click inside your image, the Color Replacement tool samples the color beneath the cross symbol at the center of the cursor. It then replaces any colors inside the brush similar to the sampled color. Photoshop determines similarity based on the Tolerance setting of the tool.

Fix Red Eye in a Photo

Y ou can fix the red eye effect that occurs in pictures taken with flash in low light by using the Red Eye tool. When applied to the eye of your subject, the tool replaces the reddish pixels in the area with pixels of a predefined color.

Fix Red Eye in a Photo

1 Click and hold the **Spot Healing Brush** tool (🖌).

2 In the list that appears, click the **Red Eye** tool (👁).

3 Type a value from 1% to 100% for Pupil Size to determine the size of the area affected.

4 Type a value from 1% to 100% for Darken Amount to determine the darkness of the applied color.

5 Click the center of a pupil.

Photoshop replaces the red pixels with a dark gray hue.

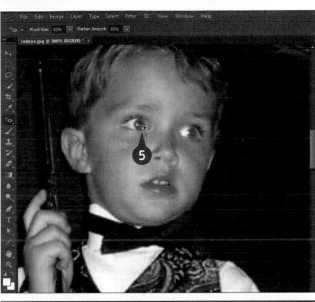

6 Click the other eye.

Photoshop fixes the other eye.

TIPS

What are alternatives to the Red Eye tool?
You can use the Color Replacement tool to fix red eye. First, select the red eye with the **Elliptical Marquee** tool (). Select a dark gray hue as your foreground color and then apply the foreground color over the eye with the **Color Replacement** tool (⬚). This can also help you fix the blue- and green-eye phenomena that can occur with animals.

What can cause problems for the Red Eye tool?
If your subject has a reddish skin tone in the photo, the Red Eye tool may apply color to more than just the eyes. To avoid this, you can first select the eyes with the Elliptical Marquee tool (⬚). Then, the Red Eye tool leaves the rest of the image alone when you apply it. See Chapter 4 for more.

CHAPTER 7

Adjusting Lighting and Colors

You can fine-tune the colors in your image — darken them, lighten them, or remove them completely. This chapter introduces the tools that do the trick.

Change Brightness and Contrast

The Brightness/Contrast command provides a way to adjust the highlights and shadows in your image. To change the brightness or contrast of small parts of your image, use the Dodge or Burn tool. See the section "Using the Dodge and Burn Tools" for more.

If you make a selection before using the Brightness/Contrast command, changes affect only the selected pixels. Similarly, if you have a multilayered image, your adjustments affect only the selected layer. For more on making selections, see Chapter 4. For more on layers, see Chapter 8.

Change Brightness and Contrast

1 Click **Image**.

2 Click **Adjustments**.

3 Click **Brightness/Contrast**.

The Brightness/Contrast dialog box opens with sliders set to 0.

4 To display your adjustments in the image window as you make them, click the **Preview** check box (■ changes to ☑).

5 Click and drag the **Brightness** slider (⬚).

Drag to the right to lighten the image, or drag to the left to darken the image.

Ⓐ You can also lighten the image by typing a number from 1 to 100 or darken the image by typing a negative number from -1 to -100.

6 Click and drag the **Contrast** slider (⬜).

Drag to the right to increase the contrast, or drag to the left to decrease the contrast.

Note: Increasing contrast can bring out details in your image; decreasing it can soften details.

Ⓑ You can also increase the contrast by typing a number from 1 to 100 or decrease the contrast by typing a negative number from -1 to -100.

7 Click **OK**.

Photoshop applies the new brightness and contrast values.

Note: You can also apply brightness and contrast adjustments to an image with an adjustment layer. For more, see Chapter 8.

TIP

How can I adjust the contrast of an image automatically?

Click **Image** and then **Auto Contrast**. This converts the lightest pixels in the image to white and the darkest pixels in the image to black. Making the highlights brighter and the shadows darker boosts the contrast, which can improve the appearance of poorly exposed photographs. In this example, you can use the Auto Contrast command to bring out the colors in a bridge scene.

Using the Dodge and Burn Tools

You can use the Dodge and Burn tools to brighten or darken specific areas of an image, respectively. You use brush strokes to apply the tools. *Dodge* is a photographic term that describes the blocking of light when printing from a film negative. *Burn* is a photographic term that describes the addition of light when printing from a film negative.

These tools are an alternative to the Brightness/Contrast command, which affects the entire image. To brighten or darken the entire image, see the section "Change Brightness and Contrast."

Using the Dodge and Burn Tools

Using the Dodge Tool

1 Click the **Dodge** tool (⬛).

2 Click here (▾) to open the Brush menu.

3 Click the brush you want to use.

Ⓐ You can also choose the range of colors you want to affect and the tool's exposure or strength.

4 Click and drag over the area that you want to lighten.

Photoshop lightens the area.

Using the Burn Tool

1 Click and hold the **Dodge** tool ().

2 Click the **Burn** tool ( ) in the list that appears.

Ⓑ You can select the brush, the range of colors you want to affect, and the tool's exposure, or strength.

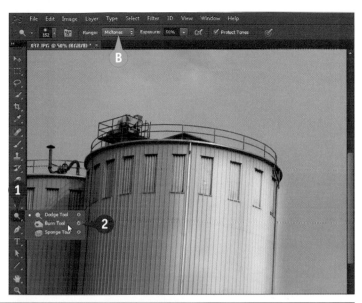

3 Click and drag over the area that you want to darken.

Photoshop darkens the area.

How do I invert the bright and dark colors in an image?

Click **Image**, **Adjustments**, and then **Invert**. This makes the image look like a film negative. Bright colors become dark — and vice versa. Applying the Invert command a second time changes the colors back to how they were originally.

How can I add extra shadows to the bottom of an object?

Applying the Burn tool ( ) with the Range set to Shadows offers a useful way to add shadows to the shaded side of an object. Likewise, you can use the Dodge tool ( ) with the Range set to Highlights to add highlights to the lighter side of an object.

Using the Blur and Sharpen Tools

You can sharpen or blur specific areas of your image with the Sharpen and Blur tools. This enables you to emphasize or de-emphasize objects in a photo. You apply the tools with brush strokes over the area you want to affect. You can change the brush size to control how much area you want to cover.

You can blur or sharpen an entire image by using one of the Blur or Sharpen commands located in Photoshop's Filter menu. For more, see Chapter 10.

Using the Blur and Sharpen Tools

Using the Blur Tool

1 Click the **Blur** tool ().

2 Click here (▾) to open the Brush menu.

3 Click the brush you want to use.

Ⓐ To change the strength of the tool, type a value from 1% to 100%.

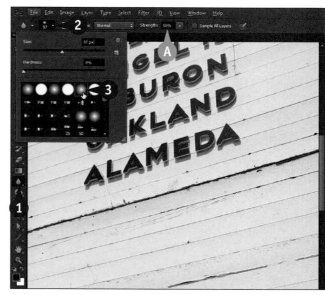

4 Click and drag an area of the image.

Photoshop blurs the area you click and drag over.

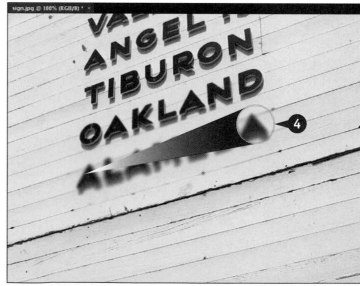

Using the Sharpen Tool

1 Click and hold the **Blur** tool ().

2 Click the **Sharpen** tool (▲) in the list that appears.

B You can type a value from 1% to 100% to set the strength of the tool.

3 Click and drag an area of the image.

Photoshop sharpens the area of the image you click and drag over.

TIP

How do I use the Smudge tool?

The Smudge tool (◪) simulates dragging a finger through wet paint, shifting colors and blurring your image.

1 Click and hold the **Blur** tool (◪).

2 Click the **Smudge** tool (◪) in the list that appears.

You can adjust the tool's brush size and strength on the Options bar.

3 Click and drag over an area of your image to smudge it.

Adjust Levels

You can use the Levels command to make fine adjustments to the highlights, midtones, or shadows in an image. Although more difficult to use, the Levels command offers more control over brightness than the Brightness/Contrast command, covered in the section "Change Brightness and Contrast."

To change only selected pixels, select them before performing the Levels command. Similarly, in a multilayered image, your adjustments affect only the selected layer.

Adjust Levels

1 Click **Image**.

2 Click **Adjustments**.

3 Click **Levels**.

The Levels dialog box opens.

4 To display your adjustments in the image window as you make them, click the **Preview** check box (☐ changes to ☑).

You can use the Input sliders to adjust an image's brightness, midtones, and highlights.

5 Click and drag ▲ to the right to darken shadows and increase contrast.

6 Click and drag ◻ to the left to lighten the bright areas of the image and increase contrast.

7 Click and drag ◻ to adjust the midtones — the shades between the shadows and highlights — of the image.

You can use the Output sliders to decrease the contrast while either lightening or darkening the image.

8 Click and drag ▲ to the right to lighten the image.

9 Click and drag △ to the left to darken the image.

10 Click **OK**.

Photoshop makes brightness and contrast adjustments to the image.

In this example, adjusting the Levels has increased the contrast to bring out detail.

Note: You can also apply levels adjustments to an image with an adjustment layer. For more, see Chapter 8.

TIP

How do I automatically adjust the brightness levels of an image?
Click **Image** and then **Auto Tone**. This converts the lightest pixels in the image to white and the darkest pixels to black. This command is similar to the Auto Contrast command and can quickly improve the contrast of an overly gray photographic image. In this example, you can use the Auto Tone command to make the colors in this photo of leaves crisper.

Adjust Curves

You can manipulate the tones and contrast of your image with the Curves dialog box. In the dialog box, a sloping line graph represents colors in the image. The top right part of the line represents the highlights, the middle part the midtones, and the bottom left the shadows.

If you make a selection before performing the Curves command, only the selected pixels are affected. Similarly, if you have a multilayered image, your adjustments affect only the selected layer. For more on making selections, see Chapter 4. For more on layers, see Chapter 8.

Adjust Curves

1 Click **Image**.

2 Click **Adjustments**.

3 Click **Curves**.

The Curves dialog box opens.

A The dialog box includes a histogram of the existing colors in the image, with the dark colors represented on the left and the light colors on the right.

4 Click the line graph and then drag to adjust the lighting in the image.

Dragging the curve up and to the left lightens the image, and dragging it down and to the right darkens it.

5 Click and drag at additional points on the line graph to fine-tune the lighting.

To boost contrast, you can create a curve with a slight S shape. This lightens the highlights, darkens the shadows, and keeps the midtones relatively unchanged.

6 Click **OK** to apply the adjustments and close the dialog box.

B To reset the line graph, you can press **Alt** and then click **Cancel**, which changes to **Reset**.

Photoshop adjusts the tones in the image.

TIP

How do I apply automatic adjustments to my image with the Curves dialog box?

The Curves dialog box offers several presets that you can select from to apply common adjustments.

1 In the Curves dialog box, click a setting in the Preset menu.

Photoshop adjusts the shape of the line graph and adjusts the colors in the image.

2 Click **OK** to apply the adjustment.

Adjust Hue and Saturation

You can change the hue to shift the component colors of an image. You can change the saturation to adjust the color intensity in an image. The Hue/Saturation command is useful for correcting old photos whose colors have shifted or have become faded.

If you make a selection before performing the Hue/Saturation command, only the selected pixels are affected. Similarly, if you have a multilayered image, your adjustments affect only the selected layer. For more on making selections, see Chapter 4. For more on layers, see Chapter 8.

Adjust Hue and Saturation

1 Click **Image**.

2 Click **Adjustments**.

3 Click **Hue/Saturation**.

The Hue/Saturation dialog box opens.

4 To display your adjustments in the image window as you make them, click the **Preview** check box (■ changes to ✓).

5 Click and drag the **Hue** slider (◉) to shift the colors in the image.

Dragging left or right shifts the colors in different — and sometimes bizarre — ways.

6 Click and drag the **Saturation** slider (⬜).

Dragging to the right or to the left increases or decreases the intensity of the image's colors, respectively.

A Clicking the **Colorize** check box (⬛ changes to ☑) partially desaturates the image and adds a single color. You can adjust the color with the sliders.

7 Click **OK**.

Photoshop makes the color adjustments to the image.

Note: You can also apply hue and saturation adjustments to an image with an adjustment layer. See Chapter 8 for more.

TIPS

How does Photoshop adjust an image's hues?

When you adjust an image's hues in Photoshop, its colors shift according to their position on the color wheel. The color wheel is a graphical way of presenting all the colors in the visible spectrum in the order they appear in a rainbow. Making adjustments with the Hue slider shifts the colors in a clockwise or counterclockwise direction around the wheel. For more details visit: http://wikipedia.org/wiki/Color_wheel.

How can the Hue/Saturation command enhance my digital photos?

Boosting the saturation can improve photos whose colors appear faded or washed out. Increasing the saturation by 10 to 20 points is often enough to enhance the colors without making them look artificially bright.

Using the Sponge Tool

You can use the Sponge tool to adjust the color saturation, or color intensity, of a specific area of an image. This can help bring out the colors in washed-out areas of photos or mute colors in areas that are too bright. You apply the Sponge tool by brushing strokes across your image. You can change the brush size to control how much area is affected.

To change the color intensity of the entire image all at once, you can adjust the saturation. See "Adjust Hue and Saturation" for details.

Using the Sponge Tool

Decrease Saturation

1 Click and hold the **Dodge** tool (⬛).

2 Click the **Sponge** tool (⬛) in the list that appears.

3 Click here (⬛) to open the Brush menu and then choose the brush you want to use.

4 Click here (⬛) to choose **Desaturate**.

5 Click and drag the mouse (○) to decrease the saturation of an area of the image.

Increase Saturation

1 Perform steps **1** to **3** under "Decrease Saturation."

2 Click here (⬍) to choose **Saturate**.

3 Click and drag the mouse (○) over an area of the image.

Photoshop increases the saturation of that area of the image.

You can adjust the strength of the Sponge tool by typing a new Flow setting from 1% to 100%.

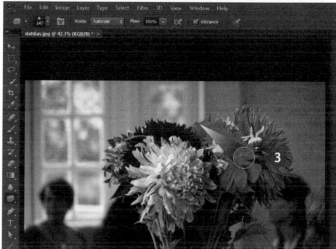

TIP

How can I easily convert a color image to a grayscale image?

1 Click **Image**.

2 Click **Adjustments**.

3 Click **Desaturate**.

Photoshop sets the saturation value of the image to 0, effectively converting it to a grayscale image.

In a multilayer image, only the selected layer is desaturated.

Note: For more control over your conversion, see the section "Convert to Black and White."

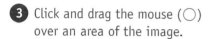

Adjust Color Balance

You can use the Color Balance command to change the amounts of specific colors in your image. This can be useful if you need to remove a colorcast introduced by a scanner or by age. Certain types of indoor lighting can also cast colors in your photos.

If you make a selection before performing the Color Balance command, only the selected pixels are affected. Similarly, if you have a multilayered image, your adjustments affect only the selected layer. For more on making selections, see Chapter 4. For more on layers, see Chapter 8.

Adjust Color Balance

1 Click **Image**.

2 Click **Adjustments**.

3 Click **Color Balance**.

The Color Balance dialog box opens.

4 To display your adjustments in the image window as you make them, click the **Preview** check box (■ changes to ☑).

5 Choose the tones in the image that you want to affect (◉ changes to ◉).

6 Click and drag a slider (◻) toward the color you want to increase.

To add a warm cast to your image, you can drag toward red or magenta.

To add a cool cast, you can drag toward blue or cyan.

7 Choose another Tone Balance option.

8 Type a number from -100 to 100 in one or more of the Color Levels fields.

Note: Step **8** is an alternative to dragging a slider.

9 Click **OK**.

Photoshop makes color adjustments to the image.

Note: You can also apply color balance adjustments to an image with an adjustment layer. See Chapter 8 for more.

TIPS

How can the Color Balance command help me improve poorly lit digital photos?
The Color Balance command can help eliminate the colorcast that can sometimes permeate a digital photo. For example, some indoor incandescent or fluorescent lighting can add a yellowish or bluish tint to your images. You can remove these tints by adding blue or red, respectively, to your images by using this command.

How can I convert my image to black and white pixels?
Click **Image**, **Adjustments**, and then **Threshold**. The Threshold dialog box opens, enabling you to control the balance of black-and-white colors in the converted image. This command makes your image look like a photocopy.

Using the Variations Command

The Variations command includes a user-friendly interface that enables you to adjust the color in your image. Image thumbnails show previews of how the image changes with different colors added. You click the thumbnails to add the colors. You can also adjust lightness in the Variations dialog box.

If you make a selection before performing the Variations command, only the selected pixels are affected. Similarly, if you have a multilayered image, your adjustments affect only the selected layer. For more on making selections, see Chapter 4. For more on layers, see Chapter 8.

Using the Variations Command

1 Click **Image**.

2 Click **Adjustments**.

3 Click **Variations**.

The Variations dialog box opens.

4 Choose a tonal range to adjust (◻ changes to ◉).

Ⓐ Alternatively, you can choose **Saturation**, or strength of color (◻ changes to ◉).

5 Click and drag the slider (◨) left to perform small adjustments or right to make large adjustments.

6 To add a color to your image, click one of the **More** thumbnails.

Ⓑ The result of the adjustments appears in the Current Pick thumbnails.

To increase the effect, you can click the **More** thumbnail again.

Ⓒ You can increase the brightness of the image by clicking **Lighter**.

Ⓓ You can decrease the brightness of the image by clicking **Darker**.

⑦ Click **OK**.

Photoshop makes the color adjustments to the image.

In this example, a yellow colorcast is added.

TIP

How can I undo color adjustments while using the Variations dialog box?

If you clicked one of the **More** thumbnail images to increase a color, you can click the **More** thumbnail image opposite to undo the effect.

When you add colors in equal amounts to an image, the colors opposite one another — for example, Green (Ⓐ) and Magenta (Ⓑ) — cancel each other out.

Clicking the Original image in the upper left corner also returns the image to its original state.

Match Colors between Images

You can use the Match Color command to match the colors in one image with the colors from another. For example, you can apply the colors from a bluish shoreline to a reddish desert to give the desert image a cooler appearance. You can also apply colors from a vibrant photo to a less colorful photo to make the less colorful photo more interesting.

If you make a selection before performing the Match Color command, only the selected pixels are affected. For more on making selections, see Chapter 4.

Match Colors between Images

1 Open a source image from which you want to match colors.

2 Open a destination image whose colors you want to change.

Make sure the image window for the destination image is selected.

3 Click **Image**.

4 Click **Adjustments**.

5 Click **Match Color**.

The Match Color dialog box opens.

6 Click here (□) to choose the filename of the source image.

7 Click and drag the sliders (📷) to control how the new colors are applied.

Luminance controls the brightness.

Color Intensity controls the saturation.

Fade controls how much color Photoshop replaces; you can increase the Fade value to greater than 0 to only partially replace the color.

8 Click **OK**.

Photoshop replaces the colors in the destination image with those in the source image.

Ⓐ In this example, Photoshop applies the reds from a photo of a glove on a baseball diamond to a less colorful photo of an industrial tank.

TIP

How do I match colors by using colors from only a selected part of my source image?
Make a selection before performing steps **3** to **5** in this section and then click the **Use Selection in Source to Calculate Colors** check box (■ changes to ☑) in the Match Color dialog box. Photoshop uses only colors from inside the selection to determine color replacement.

Correct Shadows and Highlights

You can quickly correct images with overly dark or light areas by using the Shadows/Highlights command. This command can help correct photos that have a shadowed subject because of backlighting. It can also bring out textures in bright areas of your image that appear washed out.

If you make a selection before performing the Shadows/Highlights command, only the selected pixels are affected. Similarly, if you have a multilayered image, your adjustments affect only the selected layer. For more on making selections, see Chapter 4. For more on layers, see Chapter 8.

Correct Shadows and Highlights

1 Click **Image**.

2 Click **Adjustments**.

3 Click **Shadows/Highlights**.

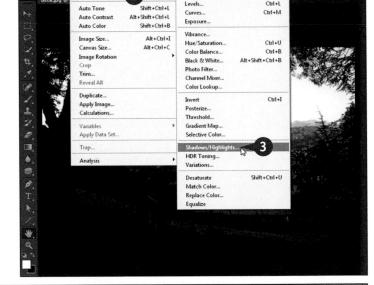

The Shadows/Highlights dialog box opens.

4 Click and drag the **Amount** slider (⬐) in the Shadows section.

The farther you drag to the right, the more the shadows lighten.

Ⓐ You can also adjust the shadows by typing a number from 0 to 100.

168

5 Click and drag the **Amount** slider () in the Highlights section.

The farther you drag to the right, the more the highlights darken.

B You can also adjust the highlights by typing a number from 0 to 100.

6 Click **OK**.

Photoshop adjusts the shadows and highlights in the image.

C Adjusting the Shadows setting brings out objects in darker areas.

D Adjusting the Highlights setting brings out objects in the lighter areas.

TIP

How do I get more control over how the Shadows/Highlights command affects my shadows and highlights?

Click the **Show More Options** check box in the Shadows/Highlights dialog box (■ changes to ☑). Additional settings appear. Adjusting the Tonal Width sliders helps you control what parts of the image are considered shadows and highlights. The Radius sliders help you control the contrast in the adjusted shadows and highlights.

Create a Duotone

For an easy way to add some color to a black-and-white photo, you can convert a grayscale image to a duotone. A *duotone* is essentially a grayscale image with a color tint. To turn a color image into a duotone, you must first remove all the color by converting it to grayscale. Then you add the tint colors one at a time.

For ways to selectively add colors to just objects in your image, see Chapter 6.

Create a Duotone

1 Click **Image**.

2 Click **Mode**.

3 Click **Grayscale**.

4 In the message box that appears, click **Discard**.

Photoshop converts your image to grayscale.

5 Click **Image**.

6 Click **Mode**.

7 Click **Duotone**.

The Duotone Options dialog box opens.

8 Click here (▾) to choose **Duotone**.

9 Click the first color swatch.

The Color Picker dialog box opens.

10 Click inside the window to choose your first duotone color.

Ⓐ You can click and drag the slider (◁▭▷) to change the color selection.

11 Click **OK**.

12 Type a name for the color.

13 Click the second color swatch.

The Color Picker dialog box opens.

14 Click inside the window to choose your second duotone color.

15 Click **OK** in the Color Picker dialog box.

16 Click **OK** in the Duotone Options dialog box.

Photoshop uses the two selected colors to create the tones in the image.

TIPS

How can I use duotones to enliven a project?
Duotones offer a quick and easy way to add color to a web page or printed publication when all you have available are grayscale images.

Can I combine more than two colors to create the tones in my grayscale image?
Yes. You can combine three colors to create a tritone or four colors to create a quadtone. Choose **Tritone** or **Quadtone** in step **7** to create these types of images. You can also choose **Monotone** to create your image tones by using a single color.

Convert to Black and White

You can use the Black and White interface to remove colors in a photo and then adjust various sliders to control the lightness and darkness of the different areas of the photo. A Preset menu gives you a variety of settings combinations with which to experiment.

If you make a selection before performing the Black & White command, only the selected pixels are affected. Similarly, if you have a multilayered image, your adjustments affect only the selected layer. For more on making selections, see Chapter 4. For more on layers, see Chapter 8.

Convert to Black and White

Adjust Lighting with Sliders

1. Click **Image**.
2. Click **Adjustments**.
3. Click **Black & White**.

The Black and White dialog box opens.

Photoshop converts your image to grayscale.

4. Click and drag a slider (🖾) to adjust the lightness of a color in the image.

The sliders correspond to the colors in the original image.

Drag to the left to darken a color.

Drag to the right to lighten a color.

Photoshop adjusts the color.

Ⓐ In this example, a kayak is darkened by clicking and dragging the **Cyans** slider to the left.

5. Click **OK** to apply the adjustments.

Adjust Lighting with the Mouse

1 With the Black and White dialog box open, click inside the image and then press and hold the mouse button ($\hookleftarrow$ changes to $\nearrow$).

B Photoshop reads the clicked color and then highlights the relevant color in the dialog box.

2 With the mouse button down, drag the cursor to the left or right to adjust the color lightness ($\nearrow$ changes to $\overset{\text{\tiny$\textcircled{}$}}{\text{}}$).

3 Click **OK** to apply the adjustment.

TIP

How can I tint my image by using the Black & White tool?

1 Click the **Tint** check box (■ changes to ☑).

Photoshop tints the image.

2 Click and drag the **Hue** slider (◙) to control the color of the tint.

A You can also click the color box to choose a tint color.

3 Click and drag the **Saturation** slider (◙) to control the intensity of the tint.

4 Click **OK**.

Adjust Vibrance

The Vibrance command can boost the intensity of the colors in an image, helping you improve the look of a faded or washed-out photo. You can also use the command to mute an overly colorful image. For another way to boost colors, see "Adjust Hue and Saturation."

If you make a selection before performing the Vibrance command, only the selected pixels are affected. Similarly, if you have a multilayered image, your adjustments affect only the selected layer. For more on making selections, see Chapter 4. For more on layers, see Chapter 8.

Adjust Vibrance

1 Click **Image**.

2 Click **Adjustments**.

3 Click **Vibrance**.

The Vibrance dialog box opens.

4 To display your adjustments in the image window as you make them, click the **Preview** check box (■ changes to ☑).

5 Click and drag the **Vibrance** slider (▣) to adjust the intensity of the colors.

The Vibrance setting takes into account the current saturation of the colors, emphasizing colors that are less intense.

6 Click and drag the **Saturation** slider (▣) to adjust the intensity of the colors in the image.

The Saturation setting changes the intensity evenly across all colors.

7 Click **OK**.

Photoshop applies the
adjustments.

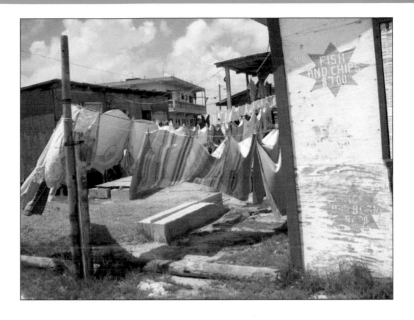

How can I improve an under- or overexposed image?

1 Click **Image**, **Adjustments**, and then **Exposure**.

2 Make exposure adjustments by dragging the
sliders (⬜).

Drag the **Exposure** slider to adjust highlights.

Drag the **Offset** slider to adjust shadows and
midtones.

Drag the **Gamma Correction** slider to adjust the
gamma brightness function, which can correct for
varying monitor brightnesses.

3 Click **OK** to apply the adjustments.

CHAPTER 8

Working with Layers

You can separate the elements in your image so that you can move and transform them independently of one another. You can accomplish this by placing them in different layers. To determine what layer elements are visible, you can rearrange the stacking order of layers or change their opacity. You can also add special layers known as adjustment layers to control the lighting, color, and other aspects of your image.

What Are Layers?

A Photoshop image can consist of multiple layers, with each layer containing different objects in the image. This enables you to edit and adjust parts of the image independently. You can select different layers in an image or change their stacking order using the Layers panel.

When you open a digital camera photo or a newly scanned image in Photoshop, it exists as a single layer known as the Background layer. You can add new layers on top of the Background layer as you work.

Layer Independence

Layered Photoshop files act like several images combined into one. Each layer of an image has its own set of pixels that you can move and transform independently of the pixels in other layers. The content of a layer can take up the entire image canvas or include just a small object within a larger image. If you want, you can place every distinct object in your image in its own layer. An image can have dozens or even hundreds of layers.

Apply Commands to Layers

Most Photoshop commands affect only the layer that you select in the Layers panel. For example, if you click and drag by using the Move tool (⊕), the selected layer moves, but the other layers stay in place. If you apply a color adjustment, only colors in the selected layer change. Putting content into layers offers a useful way to isolate the effects that you apply to your image projects. For example, by placing a fish in its own layer, you can change the color of the fish without changing the colors of the other sea creatures in your image.

Manipulate Layers

You can combine, duplicate, and hide layers in an image as well as shuffle their order. Certain parts of a layer can be hidden depending on its location in the layer stack. You can also link particular layers so they move in unison or blend content from different layers in creative ways. You manage all of this in Photoshop's Layers panel.

Transparency

Layers can have transparent areas, where the elements in the layers below can show through. When you perform a Cut or Erase command on a layer, the affected pixels become transparent. You can also make a layer partially transparent by decreasing its opacity or its fill.

Adjustment Layers

Adjustment layers are special layers that contain information about color or tonal adjustments. You can apply certain Photoshop commands, such as Levels and Curves, as adjustment layers. An adjustment layer affects the pixels in all the layers below it. You can increase or decrease an adjustment layer's intensity to get precisely the effect you want.

Save Layered Files

You can save multilayered images only in the Photoshop, PDF, and TIFF file formats. When you save such files and open them again, the arrangement of the layers is preserved. To save a layered image in another file format — for example, BMP, GIF, or JPEG — you must combine the image's layers into a single layer, a process known as *flattening*. For more on saving files, see Chapter 14.

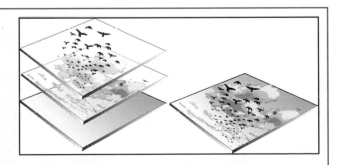

Create and Add to a Layer

To keep elements in your image independent of one another, you can create separate layers and add objects to them. Typically, you copy elements from one part of your image, or from a different image, and paste them to place them into new layers.

When you create a new layer, the layer appears in a list in the Layers panel. Layers higher in the list appear above and can cover layers lower in the list. To rearrange layers that you have created, see "Reorder Layers." To get rid of layers in your image, see "Delete a Layer."

Create and Add to a Layer

Create a Layer

1 Click the **Layers** tab to open the Layers panel.

If the Layers tab is hidden, you can click **Window** and then **Layers** to open the Layers panel.

2 Click the layer above which you want to add the new layer.

3 In the Layers panel, click the **New Layer** button (⬜).

Alternatively, you can click **Layer**, click **New**, and then click **Layer**.

A Photoshop creates a new transparent layer.

Note: To change the name of a layer, see the section "Rename a Layer."

Copy and Paste into a Layer

Note: This example shows how to add content to the new layer by copying and pasting from another image file.

1 Open another image.

2 Using a selection tool, select the content you want to copy into the other image.

Note: For more on opening an image, see Chapter 1. For more on the selection tools, see Chapter 4.

3 Click **Edit**.

4 Click **Copy**.

View the image where you created the new layer.

5 Click the new layer in the Layers panel.

6 Click **Edit**.

7 Click **Paste**.

B The selected content from the other image appears in the new layer.

TIPS

What is the Background layer?
The Background layer is the default bottom layer that appears when you create a new image that has a nontransparent background color or when you import an image from a scanner or a digital camera. You can create new layers on top of a Background layer, but not below it. Unlike other layers, a Background layer cannot contain transparent pixels.

How can I copy layers between images?
If you have multiple images open in Photoshop, you can click and drag a layer from the Layers panel of one image into the window of a different image. Photoshop copies the layer into the second image. You can move multiple layers by Ctrl +clicking (⌘+clicking on a Mac) them, and then dragging them to a different image window.

Hide a Layer

You can hide a layer to temporarily remove elements in that layer from view. Hiding a layer can be useful if you want to view or edit objects that appear in layers underneath. Hidden layers do not appear when you print or use the Save for Web command.

You can remove a layer altogether by deleting it. See "Delete a Layer" for details. Hiding a layer is different than deleting a layer because you can always make a hidden layer visible again by clicking the visibility icon in the Layers panel.

Hide a Layer

1 Click the **Layers** tab to open the Layers panel.

If the Layers tab is hidden, you can click **Window** and then **Layers** to open the Layers panel.

2 Click the visibility icon (👁) for a layer.

A The icon disappears.

Photoshop hides the layer.

To show one layer and hide all the others, you can press Alt (Option on a Mac) and then click 👁 for the layer you want to show. Pressing Alt (Option) and then clicking again makes the other layers reappear.

Note: You can also delete a layer. See the section "Delete a Layer" for more.

Move a Layer

You can use the Move tool to reposition the elements in one layer without moving those in others. You determine what layer elements move by selecting a layer in the Layers panel. Then you click and drag with the Move tool inside your image.

If you make a selection with a selection tool before using the Move command, Photoshop moves only the selected objects in the layer. For more about using selection tools, see Chapter 4. To undo a Move command, you can click **Edit** and then **Undo** or press Ctrl+Z (⌘+Z on a Mac).

Move a Layer

1 Click the **Layers** tab to open the Layers panel.

If the Layers tab is hidden, you can click **Window** and then **Layers** to open the Layers panel.

2 Click a layer.

3 Click the **Move** tool (⯈).

4 Click and drag inside the window.

Content in the selected layer moves.

Content in the other layers does not move.

Note: To move several layers at the same time, see the section "Link Layers."

183

Duplicate a Layer

By duplicating a layer, you can manipulate elements in an image while keeping a copy of their original state. Duplicating a layer creates a new layer in the Layers panel.

You can repeat the duplicate command to create many copies of objects in your image, and then use the Move command to arrange the copies. For more about moving elements in layers, see "Move a Layer."

Duplicate a Layer

1 Click the **Layers** tab to open the Layers panel.

If the Layers tab is hidden, you can click **Window** and then **Layers** to open the Layers panel.

2 Click a layer.

3 Click and drag the layer to 🗋.

Alternatively, you can click **Layer** and then **Duplicate Layer**; a dialog box opens, asking you to name the duplicate layer. You can also press `Ctrl`+`J` (`⌘`+`J` on a Mac).

A Photoshop duplicates the selected layer.

Note: To rename the duplicate layer, see the section "Rename a Layer."

B You can see that Photoshop has duplicated the layer by selecting the new layer, clicking the **Move** tool (▶), and then clicking and dragging the layer.

Delete a Layer

You can delete a layer when you no longer have a use for its contents. After deleting a layer, the layer no longer appears in the Layers panel and its content disappears from your image. An alternative to deleting a layer is to hide it. Hiding a layer keeps the layer content in your image but does not display it in the image window. For more details, see "Hide a Layer."

To undo the deletion of a layer, you can click **Edit** and then **Undo** or press `Ctrl`+`Z` (`⌘`+`Z` on a Mac).

Delete a Layer

1 Click the **Layers** tab to open the Layers panel.

If the Layers tab is hidden, you can click **Window** and then **Layers** to open the Layers panel.

2 Click a layer.

3 Click and drag the layer to the trash can icon ().

Alternatively, you can click **Layer** and then **Delete Layer** or you can select a layer and click . In both cases, a confirmation dialog box opens.

Photoshop deletes the selected layer, and the content in the layer disappears from the image window.

Note: You can also hide a layer. See the section "Hide a Layer" for more.

Reorder Layers

Layers listed in the Layers panel overlap one another depending on their stacking order. Layers higher in the list appear above layers lower in the list. You can change the stacking order of layers to move elements up or down in your image.

You can move a layer up in the Layers panel to display objects currently covered by content in layers above. If you have a layer in your image that you want to use as a background, you can move it down in the Layers panel to make it appear behind everything else.

Reorder Layers

Using the Layers Panel

1 Click the **Layers** tab to open the Layers panel.

If the Layers tab is hidden, you can click **Window** and then **Layers** to open the Layers panel.

2 Click a layer other than the Background layer.

3 Click and drag the layer to change its position in the stack.

A The layer assumes its new position in the stack.

Using the Arrange Commands

1 In the Layers panel, click a layer other than the Background layer.

2 Click **Layer**.

3 Click **Arrange**.

4 Click the command for how you want to move the layer.

You can choose **Bring to Front**, **Bring Forward**, **Send Backward**, **Send to Back**, or **Reverse**.

In this example, Bring Forward is chosen.

B The layer assumes its new position in the stack.

Note: You cannot move a layer below the default Background layer.

TIP

Are there shortcuts for changing the order of layers?

You can shift layers forward and backward in the stack by pressing the following shortcuts keys:

Move...	Windows Shortcut	Mac Shortcut
...forward one step	Ctrl +]	⌘ +]
...backward	Ctrl + [	⌘ + [
...to the very front	Shift + Ctrl +]	Shift + ⌘ +]
...to the very back	Shift + Ctrl + [	Shift + ⌘ + [

Change the Opacity of a Layer

You can adjust the opacity of a layer to let elements in the layers below show through. Opacity is the opposite of transparency — decreasing the opacity of a layer increases its transparency.

Layers can have opacities from 0 to 100 percent. A layer with an opacity of 100 percent is completely visible and obscures content that exists below it. A layer with an opacity of 0 percent is completely transparent and is not visible in your image. Another way to make a layer disappear in your image is to hide it. For details, see "Hide a Layer."

Change the Opacity of a Layer

① Click the **Layers** tab to open the Layers panel.

If the Layers tab is hidden, you can click **Window** and then **Layers** to open the Layers panel.

② Click a layer other than the Background layer.

Note: You cannot change the opacity of the Background layer.

Ⓐ The default opacity is 100%, which is completely opaque.

③ Type a new value in the Opacity field and then press Enter (Return on a Mac).

Ⓑ Alternatively, you can click ⬛ and then drag the slider (◨).

A layer's opacity can range from 0% to 100%.

Ⓒ The layer changes in opacity.

A shortcut for changing a layer's opacity is to click the layer and then press a number key.

D In this example, **3** is pressed, which changes the opacity to 30%.

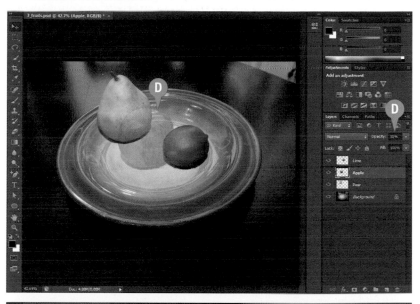

You can make multiple layers in your image semitransparent by changing their opacities.

E In this example, both the Lime and Apple layers are semitransparent.

TIP

What is the Fill setting in the Layers panel?

It is similar to the Opacity setting, except that lowering it does not affect any blending options or layer styles applied to the layer. For example, if you apply a drop shadow to a layer, lowering the Fill setting makes the layer object more transparent but does not affect the shadow behind the object. Lowering the Opacity setting does affect blending options and layer styles. For more on blending options, see the section "Blend Layers." For more on layer styles, see Chapter 9.

Merge Layers

Merging layers lets you permanently combine information from two or more separate layers. The different layers become a single layer in the Layers panel. After merging layers, you can no longer move them independently of one another. For more on moving a layer, see the section "Move a Layer." To move content in multiple layers in unison without merging the layers, you can link the layers. For details, see "Link Layers."

To undo a merge, you can click **Edit** and then **Undo** or press Ctrl+Z (⌘+Z on a Mac). For more about undoing commands, see Chapter 2.

Merge Layers

Merge Layers

1 Click the **Layers** tab to open the Layers panel.

If the Layers tab is hidden, you can click **Window** and then **Layers** to open the Layers panel.

2 Click a layer.

3 While pressing Ctrl (⌘ on a Mac), click one or more layers to merge with the selected layer.

4 Click **Layer**.

5 Click **Merge Layers**.

You can also click **Merge Down** to merge the selected layer with the layer below it or **Merge Visible** to merge all visible layers in the image.

A The layers merge.

Photoshop keeps the name of the uppermost layer. The merged layers also assume the position of the uppermost layer.

B To see the result of the merge, select the new layer, click the **Move** tool (⊹), and then click and drag the merged layer.

The elements that were previously in separate layers now move together.

Flatten an Image

1 Click **Layer**.

2 Click **Flatten Image**.

C All the layers merge into one Background layer.

D You can also access Merge and Flatten commands in the Layers panel menu. Click the panel menu (⬛) to access it.

TIPS

Why would I want to merge layers?

Merging layers enables you to save computer memory. The fewer layers a Photoshop image has, the less space it takes up in RAM and on your hard drive when you save it. Merging layers also lets you permanently combine elements of your image when you are happy with how you have arranged them relative to one another. If you want the option of rearranging all the original layers in the future, save a copy of your image before you merge layers.

What happens to layers when I save an image for the web?

When creating a JPEG, nonanimated GIF, or PNG file for publishing on the web, Photoshop automatically flattens the layers of an image before creating the new file. Your original Photoshop image retains its layers. For more on saving images, see Chapter 14.

Rename a Layer

You can rename a layer to give it a name that describes its content. For example, in a multilayered image of flowers, you can give one layer the name "red rose" and another the name "white lily."

When you create a new layer in the Layers panel, Photoshop gives it a generic name such as "Layer 1." When you duplicate a layer in the Layers panel, the duplicate layer is given the same name as the original layer with a "copy" suffix. After you create a layer or duplicate a layer, you can rename the new layer to make the name more specific.

Rename a Layer

1 Click the **Layers** tab to open the Layers panel.

If the Layers tab is hidden, you can click **Window** and then **Layers** to open the Layers panel.

2 Click a layer.

3 Click **Layer**.

4 Click **Rename Layer**.

5 Type a new name for the layer.

6 Click outside of the text field.

A The name of the layer changes in the Layers panel.

You can also double-click the name of the layer in the Layers panel to edit the name.

Transform a Layer

You can use a transform tool to change the shape of the objects in a layer. When you transform a layer, the rest of your image remains unchanged.

Transforming can resize a layer to give it greater or lesser emphasis in your image. You can also transform a layer to stretch it horizontally or vertically. Remember that increasing the size of a layer too much can reduce the quality of the layer, especially in smaller images.

Transform a Layer

1 Click the **Layers** tab to open the Layers panel.

If the Layers tab is hidden, you can click **Window** and then **Layers** to open the Layers panel.

2 Click **Edit**.

3 Click **Transform**.

4 Click a transform command.

You can also click the **Move** tool (🖐) and then click **Show Transform Controls** on the Options bar.

5 Click and drag the side and corner handles (☐) to transform the shape of the layer (👆 changes to ↗).

6 Click ✔ or press **Enter** (⌘+**Return** on a Mac) to apply the change.

🅐 You can click ⊘ or press **Esc** to cancel the change.

Photoshop changes your image according to the transform command you selected.

Note: For more on transforming your images, see Chapter 5.

Create a Solid Fill Layer

You can create a solid fill layer to place an opaque layer of color throughout your image. You can use fill layers behind layers containing objects to create all kinds of color effects in your photos.

When you create a solid fill layer, a Color Picker dialog box appears, enabling you to select a color for the fill layer. The dialog box also enables you to select a blend mode and opacity. For more about these settings, see "Blend Layers" and "Change the Opacity of a Layer."

Create a Solid Fill Layer

1 Click the **Layers** tab to open the Layers panel.

If the Layers tab is hidden, you can click **Window** and then **Layers** to open the Layers panel.

2 Click the layer above which you want to add solid color.

3 Click **Layer**.

4 Click **New Fill Layer**.

5 Click **Solid Color**.

Ⓐ You can also click the **Create New Fill or Adjustment Layer** button (⬤) and then choose **Solid Color**.

The New Layer dialog box opens.

6 Type a name for the layer.

Ⓑ You can specify a blend mode or opacity setting for the layer.

Note: See the section "Blend Layers" or "Change the Opacity of a Layer" for more.

7 Click **OK**.

The Color Picker dialog box opens.

8 To change the range of colors that appears in the window, click and drag the slider (▭).

9 To choose a fill color, click in the color field.

10 Click **OK**.

C Photoshop creates a new layer filled with a solid color.

Layers below the new fill layer are covered, whereas the layers above the new layer are not affected.

TIPS

How do I add solid color to just part of a layer?
Make a selection with a selection tool before creating the solid fill layer. Photoshop adds color only inside the selection.

What other types of fill layers can I create?
You can add a gradient fill layer that shows a transition from one color to another by clicking **Layer**, **New Fill Layer**, and then **Gradient**. You can add a pattern fill layer that displays a repeated design by clicking **Layer**, **New Fill Layer**, and then **Pattern**.

Create an Adjustment Layer

Adjustment layers enable you to store color and tonal changes in a layer instead of having them permanently applied to your image. The information in an adjustment layer is applied to the pixels in the layers below it. By changing the opacity of an adjustment layer, you can control the amount of changes applied. You can also hide an adjustment layer to turn the changes off completely.

You can use adjustment layers to test an editing technique without applying it to the original layer. Adjustment layers are especially handy for experimenting with colors, tones, and brightness settings.

Create an Adjustment Layer

① Click the **Layers** tab to open the Layers panel.

If the Layers tab is hidden, you can click **Window** and then **Layers** to open the Layers panel.

② Click the **Adjustments** tab to open the Adjustments panel.

If a panel tab is not visible, you can click **Window** and then the panel name to open the panel.

③ Click the layer above which you want to create an adjustment layer.

④ Click an adjustment layer button.

Note: See the tip on the next page for a description of the adjustment types.

Ⓐ Photoshop opens the Properties panel for the adjustment layer.

Ⓑ Photoshop places the new adjustment layer above the selected layer.

Ⓒ You can specify a blend mode or opacity setting for the layer.

Note: See the section "Blend Layers" or "Change the Opacity of a Layer" for more.

196

D The settings for the adjustment command appear in the Properties panel.

5 Click and drag the sliders (⬚) or type values to adjust the settings.

In this example, an adjustment layer is created that changes the hue and saturation.

6 Click here to close the Properties panel.

Photoshop applies the effect to the layers below the adjustment layer, including the Background layer.

E In this example, the adjustment layer affects the three layers below it while leaving the Lime layer above it unaffected.

7 You can click the Properties button (⬚) to show a list of adjustment settings again.

Edit an Adjustment Layer

You can modify the color and tonal changes that you defined in an adjustment layer. This enables you to fine-tune your adjustment layer to get the effect you want.

You can decrease the opacity of an adjustment layer to lessen its effect on the layers below it. You can also turn off an adjustment layer completely in the Layers panel.

Edit an Adjustment Layer

1 Click the **Layers** tab to open the Layers panel.

If the Layers tab is hidden, you can click **Window** and then **Layers** to open the Layers panel.

2 Double-click the adjustment layer thumbnail you want to edit.

The Properties panel opens showing the settings corresponding to the adjustment command.

3 Click and drag the sliders (🔲) to change the settings in the panel.

Photoshop applies your changes.

In this example, the hue and saturation are changed, which shifts the color in the layers below the adjustment layer.

Ⓐ You can lessen the effect of an adjustment layer by decreasing the layer's opacity to less than 100%.

④ Click here to close the Properties panel.

Ⓑ In this example, the opacity was decreased to 40%, which reverses the decrease in saturation. Some of the original color in the fruit returns.

Ⓒ You can drag the adjustment layer to the trash can (🗑) to delete it.

TIP

How do I merge an adjustment layer with a regular layer?

❶ Place the adjustment layer above the layer with which you want to merge it.

❷ Click **Layer** and then **Merge Down**.

Photoshop applies the adjustment layer's effects permanently to the layer below it. The adjustment layer is removed from the Layers panel.

Link Layers
Select Linked Layers

Merge Down ❷   Ctrl+E
Merge Visible   Shift+Ctrl+E
Flatten Image

Matting   ▶

Apply an Adjustment-Layer Preset

Photoshop offers a variety of ready-to-use adjustment layers that apply common color-correction techniques and special effects. After you apply them, you can make changes to their settings in the Adjustments panel.

The presets are often a good first step in applying color and tonal adjustments to your image.

Apply an Adjustment-Layer Preset

1 Click the **Layers** tab to open the Layers panel.

If the Layers tab is hidden, you can click **Window** and then **Layers** to open the Layers panel.

2 Click the **Adjustments** tab to open the Adjustments panel.

If a panel tab is not visible, you can click **Window** and then the panel name to open the panel.

3 Click the layer above which you want to create an adjustment layer.

4 Click an Adjustment layer button to open the Properties panel.

See "Create an Adjustment Layer" for a list of the types of adjustments you can apply.

Ⓐ Photoshop creates a new adjustment layer.

Ⓑ The settings appear in the Properties panel.

❺ Click here to choose a preset.

The settings affect the layers below the adjustment layer, including the Background layer.

❻ Click here to close the Properties panel.

TIP

How do I save an adjustment layer as a preset?

❶ Create an adjustment layer and then select it.

❷ Click the panel menu (▤) in the Properties panel.

❸ Click **Save Preset**. The command name differs depending on the type of adjustment layer you are saving.

The Save dialog box opens, enabling you to name and save the preset.

After saving, your preset appears in the Adjustments panel preset list.

Link Layers

Linking causes different layers to move in unison when you drag them with the Move tool. You may find linking useful when you want to keep elements of an image aligned with one another but do not want to merge their layers. Keeping layers unmerged enables you to apply effects to each layer independently.

See the section "Merge Layers" for more on merging. For more on moving a layer, see the section "Move a Layer." When you select a layer in the Layers panel, a link icon indicates any other layers linked to that layer.

Link Layers

Create a Link

1 Click the **Layers** tab to open the Layers panel.

If the Layers tab is hidden, you can click **Window** and then **Layers** to open the Layers panel.

2 While pressing and holding **Ctrl** (⌘ on a Mac), click the layers you want to link.

3 Click **Layer**.

4 Click **Link Layers**.

Ⓐ Doing so turns on a linking icon (🔗).

The layers link together.

Ⓑ You can also click **Link Layers** (🔗) in the Layers panel.

Move Linked Layers

1 Click the **Move** tool ().

2 Click and drag inside the image window.

The linked layers move together.

Unlink Layers

1 While pressing Ctrl (⌘ on a Mac), click the layers you want to unlink.

2 Click **Layer**.

3 Click **Unlink Layers**.

Photoshop removes the link.

TIP

How do I keep from changing a layer after I have it the way I want it?
You can lock the layer by selecting the layer and then clicking the **Lock All** icon () in the Layers panel. You cannot move, delete, or otherwise edit a locked layer. You can click the **Lock Transparent Pixels** icon () to prevent a user from editing the transparent pixels in the layer. Click the **Lock Image Pixels** icon () to lock the nontransparent pixels in a layer, and click the **Lock Position** icon () to keep a layer from moving.

Blend Layers

You can use the blending modes in Photoshop Elements to specify how pixels in a layer should blend with the layers below. You can blend layers to create all kinds of visual effects in your photos. In the following example, two photos are combined in one image file as two separate layers, and then layers are blended together.

When you create a new layer, the default blending mode is Normal, which applies no special blending to the layer. If you make changes to the blending mode, switching back to Normal removes any blending effects.

Blend Layers

Blend a Regular Layer

1 Click the **Layers** tab to open the Layers panel.

If the Layers tab is hidden, you can click **Window** and then **Layers** to open the Layers panel.

2 Click the layer that you want to blend.

3 Click here (⊡) to choose a blend mode.

Photoshop blends the selected layer with the layers below it.

This example blends a sunset layer with a layer of a surfer by using the Hard Light mode.

Blend an Adjustment Layer

1 Click the **Layers** tab to open the Layers panel.

If the Layers tab is hidden, you can click **Window** and then **Layers** to open the Layers panel.

2 Click the adjustment layer that you want to blend.

3 Click here (🔽) to choose a blend mode.

Photoshop blends the selected layer with the layers below it.

This example shows the Exclusion mode applied to a Hue/Saturation adjustment layer, which creates a photo-negative effect where the layers overlap.

TIP

What effects do some of the different blending modes have?
- Multiply: Darkens the colors where the selected layer overlaps layers below it.
- Screen: The opposite of Multiply. It lightens colors where layers overlap.
- Color: Takes the selected layer's colors and blends them with the details in the layers below it.
- Luminosity: The opposite of Color. It takes the selected layer's details and mixes them with the colors below it.

Work with Smart Objects

You can convert a layer into a Smart Object. Unlike a regular layer, Photoshop remembers the original composition of a Smart Object, so you can resize and perform other operations on it without its quality degrading.

Smart Object layers are designated with a special badge in the Layers panel.

Work with Smart Objects

Create a Smart Object

1 Click the layer you want to convert into a Smart Object.

2 Click **Layer**.

3 Click **Smart Objects**.

4 Click **Convert to Smart Object**.

Ⓐ Photoshop converts the layer to a Smart Object.

Smart Objects are designated with a special badge (⊞) in the Layers panel.

Duplicate a Smart Object

1️⃣ Click a Smart Object in the Layers panel.

2️⃣ Click **Layer**.

3️⃣ Click **Smart Objects**.

4️⃣ Click **New Smart Object via Copy**.

Ⓑ Photoshop duplicates the Smart Object, and the new Smart Object appears in the Layers panel.

5️⃣ Click the **Move** tool (◤).

6️⃣ Click and drag to view the new Smart Object.

TIP

How do I convert a Smart Object back to a regular layer?

1️⃣ Click the Smart Object in the Layers panel.

2️⃣ Click **Layer** and then **Smart Objects**.

3️⃣ Click **Rasterize**.

Photoshop converts the Smart Object back to a layer.

Because Photoshop remembers the original composition of a Smart Object, you can transform the object multiple times without it degrading in quality like a normal object would. This makes Smart Objects useful for elements in your image that you want to resize and otherwise experiment with.

Work with Smart Objects (continued)

Scale a Smart Object

① Click the Smart Object in the Layers panel.

② Click **Edit**.

③ Click **Transform**.

④ Click **Scale**.

A rectangular bounding box with handles (□) on the sides and corners surrounds the object.

⑤ Click and drag the handles (□) to shrink the object (⍟ changes to ⤢).

⑥ Click ✓ or press **Enter** (⌘+**Return** on a Mac) to commit the scaling.

Ⓐ Photoshop shrinks the object.

7 Repeat steps **2** to **4**.

8 Click and drag the handles (☐) to enlarge the object (↖ changes to ↗).

9 Click ✓ or press **Enter** (⌘+ **Return** on a Mac) to commit the scaling.

Ⓑ Photoshop enlarges the object.

Because Photoshop remembers the pixel information associated with the original object, the quality of the Smart Object is not degraded when you rescale it to its original size.

TIP

How can I insert another image into my project as a Smart Object?

You can use the Place command to insert a separate image as a Smart Object:

1 Click **File** and then **Place**.

2 In the Place dialog box that opens, click the image file you want to use.

3 Click **Place**.

4 Press **Enter** (**Return** on a Mac) to complete the Place command. Photoshop adds the image as a Smart Object.

Create a Layer Group

You can create a layer group to organize related layers together in the Layers panel. By selecting a layer group, you can execute commands on all the layers in the group at once. For example, you can hide, show, move, or reorder the layers in a layer group.

Layer groups act similarly to folders in a file system insofar as you can easily move files in a folder from one place to another.

Create a Layer Group

Create a Layer Group

1 Click a layer in the Layers panel.

2 Click **Create a New Group** (🗀).

Ⓐ Photoshop creates a layer group above the selected layer.

You can double-click the layer group text to rename the layer group.

Add to a Layer Group

1 Click and drag a layer in the Layers panel to the layer group.

To add multiple layers at once, you can Ctrl +click to select the layers before dragging.

2 Release the mouse button.

B Photoshop adds the layer to the group.

C You can repeat steps **1** and **2** to add more layers to the group.

Execute Commands on a Layer Group

1 Click a layer group.

2 Click the visibility icon (👁).

D Photoshop hides all the layers in the layer group.

E You can click the **Move** tool (✥) to move all the layers in a selected layer group.

F You can click here (▼) to close the layer group to free up space in the Layers panel (▼ changes to ▶).

TIPS

How do I delete a layer group?
You can click a layer group in the Layers panel and then click 🗑. A dialog box opens, enabling you to delete the group and all of its contents or just the group.

How can I control the opacity of several layers at once?
You can add the layers to a layer group, select the group, and then change the opacity of the group just as you would a single layer. For more, see the section "Change the Opacity of a Layer."

Filter Layers

You can filter layers in the Layers panel to show only layers of a certain name, type, or other criteria. This can be useful if you have dozens or even hundreds of layers in an image project. For example, you might want to display only type layers if you are interested in editing the words and other text in your image. You can filter out other types of layers such as shape and adjustment layers.

Layer filtering is a new feature in Photoshop CS6.

Filter Layers

Create a Filter

1 Open an image with multiple layers.

2 Click **Window** and then **Layers** to open the Layers panel.

3 Click ▤ to select a filter type.

4 Adjust the filter criteria.

You may need to type text, select from a menu, or click a button, depending on the filter type.

Ⓐ Photoshop filters the layers in the Layers panel, displaying only the ones matching the criteria.

In this example, only layers with the Stroke effect applied to them appear.

Turn Off a Filter

① Click ▣ (▣ changes to ▣).

Photoshop turns off the filter and displays all the layers in the image.

What are some different kinds of filters?
With the Kind type selected in the Layers panel, you can click buttons to filter the following types:

▦	Display only the regular pixel layers.
◕	Display only adjustment layers.
T	Display only type layers.
◫	Display only shape layers.
▨	Display only Smart Object layers.

Add a Layer Mask

You can apply a layer mask to a layer to precisely control what pixels in the layer are shown and what pixels are hidden. You define the mask by applying colors using Photoshop tools. A white color in the mask defines what in the layer is visible. Applying black to the layer mask with a brush or other tool specifies what parts of the layer are hidden. You can also apply shades of gray to partially show content in the layer. When you add a layer mask to a layer, Photoshop adds a mask icon next to the regular layer icon in the Layers panel.

Add a Layer Mask

1 Click the **Layers** tab to open the Layers panel.

If the Layers tab is hidden, you can click **Window** and then **Layers** to open the Layers panel.

2 Click the layer to which you want to apply the mask.

3 Click **Add Layer Mask** (■).

You can alternatively click **Layer**, click **Layer Mask**, and then click **Reveal All** or click **Hide All**. This creates an all-white or all-black layer mask, respectively.

Ⓐ Photoshop adds a layer mask icon to the layer.

The new layer mask is completely white, which means the mask hides none of the layer.

Ⓑ The foreground and background colors change to white and black, respectively.

4 Click the **Brush** tool (✏).

5 Click 🔽 and set the brush size and shape.

214

Note: For more about using the Brush tool, see Chapter 6.

6 Using a black color, click and drag on the part of the layer you want to hide.

C The brush applies a black color to the mask.

D Photoshop hides the pixels where the mask is black in color.

7 Click the foreground color (☐) and select a shade of gray in the Color Picker that appears.

Note: See Chapter 6 for more about selecting colors.

8 Click and drag on the part of the layer that you want to partially hide.

E The brush applies a gray color to the mask.

F Photoshop turns the masked pixels partially transparent.

Darker gray colors obscure the layer's content more than lighter gray colors.

TIPS

How do I paint colors onto layer content that has a mask?
To apply color normally to a layer that has a layer mask, click the regular layer icon in the Layers panel, then apply color with the Brush or other tool. If the layer mask icon is selected rather than the regular layer icon, the painted colors are applied to the mask.

After I have my layer mask exactly how I want it, how do I apply it permanently to the layer?
Right-click the layer mask icon in the Layers panel and select **Apply Layer Mask** from the menu that appears. Photoshop applies the mask to the layer, permanently removing the pixels that the mask has hidden. The layer mask is removed from the layer.

Edit a Layer Mask

A layer mask offers a convenient tool for editing images because it hides pixels in your image instead of deleting them. You can reveal pixels that were previously hidden, or hide more pixels, by editing the colors in the mask.

To unhide a masked part of an image, you can paint a white color on the mask using the Brush tool. To hide more of your layer, you can paint on the mask using a black color. By zooming in to edges in your image, you can carefully edit the mask and display just the layer content that you want shown.

Edit a Layer Mask

① Add a layer mask to a layer in your image.

Note: See "Add a Layer Mask" for more information.

② Click the layer mask icon for the layer you want to edit.

③ Click the foreground color (☐) and set it to white using the Color Picker that appears.

Note: See Chapter 6 for more on setting the foreground color.

④ Click to select the **Brush** tool (▨).

⑤ Click and drag on the hidden part of the layer you want to appear.

Ⓐ The brush applies a white color to the mask.

Ⓑ Photoshop reveals the pixels where the mask is painted white.

⑥ Click the **Zoom** tool (🔍).

⑦ Click **Zoom In** (🔍).

⑧ Click to magnify the part of the masked layer that you want to edit.

⑨ Click the **Brush** tool (✏️).

⑩ Click the foreground color and set it to black using the Color Picker that appears.

⑪ Click and drag on the visible part of the layer that you want hidden.

Ⓒ The brush applies a black color to the mask and hides content in that area of the mask.

Note: When applying colors to the layer mask, remember that white reveals and black conceals.

TIP

Are there other ways to view the layer masks that I apply?
With the masked layer selected in the Layers panel, press \, which is located above Enter on most keyboards. Photoshop displays the mask as a transparent red color, called a *rubylith*, over your image. To turn off the rubylith, press \ again. You can display the mask as a black-and-white image by pressing and holding Alt (Option on a Mac) and clicking the layer mask icon for the layer. To turn off the black-and-white view, click the layer icon. You can edit your mask while in the rubylith or black-and-white mode by painting on the mask.

CHAPTER 9

Applying Layer Styles

You can apply special effects to layers by using Photoshop's built-in layer styles. With these styles, you can add shadows, glows, and 3-D appearances to your layers. Photoshop's Styles panel enables you to easily apply predefined combinations of styles to your image or create your own styles.

Apply a Drop Shadow

You can apply a drop shadow to make a layer appear to float above the canvas. You can control many aspects of your drop shadow, including its opacity, distance, color, and angle. To make the shadow more subtle you can lower its opacity and distance from the layer to which it is applied.

A drop shadow can be added to text as well as objects in a layer. For more on working with text, see Chapter 12. For more about layers, see Chapter 8.

Apply a Drop Shadow

1 Click the **Layers** tab to open the Layers panel.

If the Layers tab is hidden, you can click **Window** and then **Layers** to open the Layers panel.

2 Click the layer to which you want to add the effect.

3 Click **Layer**.

4 Click **Layer Style**.

5 Click **Drop Shadow**.

Ⓐ You can also click the **Add a Layer Style** button (fx) and then choose **Drop Shadow** from the menu.

The Layer Style dialog box opens.

Note: Perform steps **6** to **11** if you want to enter your own settings. If you want to use the default settings, you can skip to step **12**.

6 Type an Opacity value to specify the shadow's transparency.

7 Click the color swatch to select a shadow color.

Note: The default shadow color is black.

8 Type an Angle value to specify in which direction the shadow is cast.

9 Type a Distance value to specify how far the shadow is displaced.

10 Type a Spread value to specify the fuzziness of the shadow's edge.

11 Type a Size value to specify the size of the shadow's edge.

You can also drag a slider (⬚) to change the Distance, Spread, and Size values.

12 Click **OK**.

B Photoshop creates a shadow in back of the selected layer.

C Photoshop displays the name of the style under the affected layer in the Layers panel.

Note: In this example, the effect is applied to a text layer. For more on text, see Chapter 12.

TIP

How do I add an inner shadow to a layer?

An inner shadow creates a *cutout* effect, with the selected layer appearing to drop behind the image canvas:

1 Click a layer in the Layers panel.

2 Click **Layer**, **Layer Style**, and then **Inner Shadow**.

A Photoshop applies the style to objects in the layer. You can adjust the inner shadow in the Layer Style dialog box that opens.

Apply an Outer Glow

The Outer Glow effect adds faint coloring to the outside edge of a layer's content, which can help highlight the layer. The effect can give an object in your image a ghostly or electric look and feel depending on the color and size of the outer glow.

Photoshop offers various preset outer glow styles. You can also fine-tune your Outer Glow settings by adjusting the color, size, opacity, and other options to create a specific look.

Apply an Outer Glow

1. Click the **Layers** tab to open the Layers panel.

   If the Layers tab is hidden, you can click **Window** and then **Layers** to open the Layers panel.

2. Click the layer to which you want to add the style.

3. Click **Layer**.

4. Click **Layer Style**.

5. Click **Outer Glow**.

   Ⓐ You can also click the **Add a Layer Style** button (🗔) and then choose **Outer Glow**.

   The Layer Style dialog box opens.

Note: Perform steps **6** to **10** if you want to enter your own Outer Glow settings. If you want to use the default settings, you can skip to step **11**.

6. Type an Opacity value to specify the glow's darkness.

7. Specify a Noise value to add speckling to the glow.
   You can also drag the sliders (🔘) to change the Opacity and Noise values.

8. Click the color swatch to choose the color of the glow (🔘 changes to 🔘).

   Ⓑ You can also choose from a series of preset color gradients by clicking here (🔽).

9 Type a Spread value to determine the fuzziness of the glow.

10 Type a Size value to specify the size of the glow.

You can also drag the sliders () to change the spread and size values.

11 Click **OK**.

C Photoshop creates a glow around the outer edge of objects in the selected layer.

D Photoshop displays the name of the style under the affected layer in the Layers panel.

TIP

How do I give elements in a layer an inner glow?
The Inner Glow style adds color to the inside edge of a layer. To apply it, follow these steps:

1 Click a layer in the Layers panel.

2 Click **Layer**, **Layer Style**, and then **Inner Glow**.

A Photoshop applies the style to objects in the layer.

Apply Beveling and Embossing

You can bevel and emboss a layer to give it a three-dimensional look. This can make objects in the layer stand out and seem to rise off or sink into the screen. Beveling and Embossing can be especially useful when placing a title or caption over a photograph or other complex image, because it can help separate your text from the image behind it.

You can also use a drop shadow to help your text stand out clearly. See "Apply a Drop Shadow" for details.

Apply Beveling and Embossing

1 Click the **Layers** tab to open the Layers panel.

If the Layers tab is hidden, you can click **Window** and then **Layers** to open the Layers panel.

2 Click the layer to which you want to add the style.

3 Click **Layer**.

4 Click **Layer Style**.

5 Click **Bevel & Emboss**.

A You can also click the **Add a Layer Style** button (⏢) and then choose **Bevel & Emboss**.

The Layer Style dialog box opens.

Note: Perform steps **6** to **9** if you want to enter your own settings. If you want to use the default settings, you can skip to step **10**.

6 Click here (⬛) to choose an effect style.

Choosing Inner Bevel creates a three-dimensional look.

7 Specify the direction of the style's shadowing (◯ changes to ◉).

8 Type Depth and Size values to control the magnitude of the style.

224

9 Specify the direction of the shading by changing the Angle and Altitude values.

B You can click here (⬛) to choose one of the Gloss Contour settings to apply abstract styles to your layer.

10 Click **OK**.

C Photoshop applies the Bevel and Emboss settings to the layer.

D Photoshop displays the name of the style under the affected layer in the Layers panel.

Note: In this example, the style is applied to a text layer. For more on text, see Chapter 12.

TIPS

When would I use the Bevel & Emboss style?
The style can be useful for creating three-dimensional buttons for web pages or multimedia applications. For example, to create a 3-D button, you can apply Bevel & Emboss to a colored rectangle and then add type over it.

How does the Fill setting work in the Layers panel?
Reducing a layer's Fill setting to less than 100% makes layer content transparent but keeps any styles in full effect. This is in contrast to lowering the opacity, which makes content transparent and also decreases the effect of any styles.

Apply Multiple Styles to a Layer

You can apply multiple styles to layers in your image. This enables you to enhance the look of your layers in complex ways. By carefully adjusting the setting of each style you apply, you can ensure that the styles work smoothly together to create the effect you want.

See the tip below for a quick way to turn off the effects of individual styles so that you can easily view them separately. See "Edit a Layer Style" in this chapter for more on how to fine-tune your styles.

Apply Multiple Styles to a Layer

Apply the First Style

1 Click the **Layers** tab to open the Layers panel.

If the Layers tab is hidden, you can click **Window** and then **Layers** to open the Layers panel.

2 Click the layer to which you want to add the style.

3 Click **Layer**.

4 Click **Layer Style**.

5 Click the name of the first style you want to apply.

In this example, Color Overlay is applied to the layer.

The Layer Style dialog box opens.

6 Specify the settings for the first style.

Apply the Second Style

1 Click the check box for the next style you want to apply (☐ changes to ☑).

In this example, the Outer Glow style is also applied to the layer, with the Technique set to Softer.

2 Specify the settings for this style.

You can apply other styles to the layer by repeating steps **1** and **2**.

3 Click **OK**.

Ⓐ Photoshop applies the styles to the layer.

Ⓑ The effects appear below the selected layer in the Layers panel.

TIPS

How do I turn off layer effects that I have applied?

When you apply a style to a layer, Photoshop adds the style to the Layers panel. You may have to click ▾ to see a layer's effects. You can temporarily turn off an effect by clicking the visibility icon (👁) in the Layers panel. You can turn the effect on by clicking the now-empty box again to make 👁 reappear.

Is there a quick way to remove the styles from a layer?

Select the layer and then click **Layer**, **Layer Style**, and **Clear Layer Style**. Photoshop removes all the styles currently applied to the layer.

Edit a Layer Style

You can edit a layer style that you have applied to your image. This enables you to fine-tune the effect to achieve the appearance you want. This is especially helpful if you have applied multiple layer styles to your image and need to achieve a specific look and feel. See "Apply Multiple Styles to a Layer" earlier in this chapter for more information.

Edit a Layer Style

1 Click the **Layers** tab to open the Layers panel.

If the Layers tab is hidden, you can click **Window** and then **Layers** to open the Layers panel.

In this example, the color overlay of a layer object is edited.

2 Click the layer that has the style you want to edit.

3 Click **Layer**.

4 Click **Layer Style**.

5 Click the style you want to edit.

A You can also double-click the style's name in the Layers panel.

The Layer Style dialog box opens.

B Photoshop displays the current configuration values for the style.

6 Edit the values in the Layer Style dialog box.

This example changes a color overlay.

C You can click another checked style in the Layer Style list to edit the style.

7 Click **OK**.

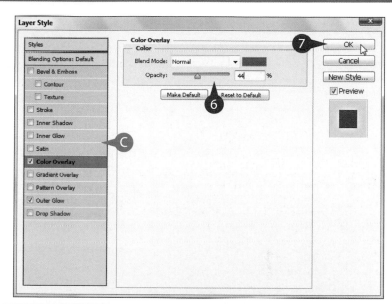

D Photoshop applies the edited style to the layer.

You can edit a style as many times as you want.

TIPS

How do I keep a layer effect from accidentally being changed?

You can lock a layer and its styles by selecting the layer and then clicking the **Lock** icon (🔒) in the Layers panel; the button depresses and becomes highlighted. The layer is then locked, which means you cannot change its styles or apply additional Photoshop commands to it. You can click the Lock icon again to unlock the layer.

Can I copy styles between layers?

Yes. Select the layer you want to copy from and then click **Layer**, **Layer Styles**, and **Copy Layer Style**. To paste the style, select the destination layer and then click **Layer**, **Layer Styles**, and **Paste Layer Style**. You can also press **Alt** (**Option** on a Mac) and then click and drag a style from one layer to another in the Layers panel to copy it.

Using the Styles Panel

You can apply a custom combination of Photoshop styles to a layer to give it a colorful or textured look. The Styles panel offers an easy way to apply such complex effects. After you apply a style combination, you can edit the individual styles to further customize the look and feel.

You can access different categories of styles through the panel menu. Categories include button styles, text effects, and textures.

Using the Styles Panel

Apply a Style from the Styles Panel

1 Click the **Layers** tab to open the Layers panel.

If the Layers tab is hidden, you can click **Window** and then **Layers** to open the Layers panel.

2 Click the **Styles** tab to display Photoshop's styles.

If the Styles tab is hidden, you can click **Window** and then **Styles** to open the Styles panel.

3 Click the layer to which you want to apply the style.

4 Click a style.

A Photoshop applies the style to the selected layer.

B The style appears as a set of effects in the Layers panel.

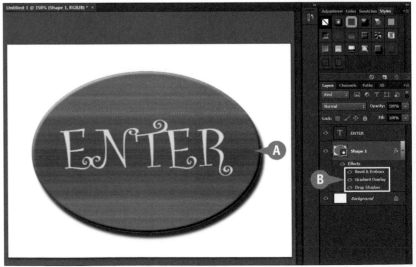

Access More Styles

1. Click the **Panel menu** icon (□).

2. Click a set of styles.

A dialog box opens to ask if you want to replace the current styles with the new set or append the new set.

3. Click **OK** or **Append**.

C Photoshop places the new styles in the Styles panel.

In this example, the new styles have been appended to the current ones.

TIP

How do I create my own custom styles?

1. Perform the techniques covered in this chapter to apply one or more effects to a layer in your image.

2. Select the layer in the Layers panel.

3. Click □ and then choose **New Style**.

4. In the New Style dialog box that opens, type a name for your new style.

5. Click **OK**.

A Your new style appears in the Styles panel.

CHAPTER 10

Applying Filters

With Photoshop's filters, you can quickly and easily apply enhancements to your image, including artistic effects, texture effects, and distortions. Filters can help you disguise defects in your images or enable you to turn a photograph into something resembling an impressionist painting. Photoshop comes with more than 100 filters; this chapter highlights only a few. For more on all the filters, see the help documentation.

Turn an Image into a Painting

You can use many of Photoshop's artistic filters to make your image look as though it was created with a paintbrush. The Dry Brush filter, for example, applies a painted effect by converting similarly colored areas in your image to solid colors. The Palette Knife filter creates a similar but softer effect. The Colored Pencil filter applies a layer of crosshatched color to your image using the current background color.

The Dry Brush filter uses the Filter Gallery interface. For more on the Filter Gallery, see the section "Apply Multiple Filters."

Turn an Image into a Painting

1 Select the layer to which you want to apply the filter.

In this example, the image has a single Background layer.

To apply the filter to just part of your image, make a selection with a selection tool.

Note: For more on layers, see Chapter 8. For more on the selection tools, see Chapter 4.

2 Click **Filter**.

3 Click **Filter Gallery**.

The Filter Gallery dialog box opens.

4 Click **Artistic** to display the Artistic filters (▶ changes to ▼).

5 Click **Dry Brush**.

Ⓐ You can also select a different filter by clicking ▼ in the right pane.

6 Fine-tune the filter effect by typing values for Brush Size, Brush Detail, and Texture.

Ⓑ You can also move the sliders (◧) to choose values.

C You can close the middle
pane by clicking ⊼.

On a Mac, you can close the
middle pane by clicking ▼
(▼ changes to ▲).

This example shows how to
thicken the Dry Brush effect
by increasing Brush Size and
decreasing Brush Detail.

7 Click **OK**.

Photoshop applies the filter.

What does the Sponge filter do?
The Sponge filter reduces detail and modifies the
shapes in an image to create the effect you get
when applying a damp sponge to a wet painting.
Apply it by opening the Filter Gallery and clicking
Artistic and then **Sponge**. This effect is different
from that of the Sponge tool (🌊), which changes
the intensity of colors in an image. See Chapter 7
for more on the Sponge tool.

**How can I make the objects in my image look
like they are molded from plastic?**
The Plastic Wrap filter gives objects a shiny
appearance, as if wrapped in heat-shrink plastic. To
apply this effect, open the Filter Gallery and click
Artistic and then **Plastic Wrap**. You can adjust how
well the plastic wrap reflects light, its shininess,
and its smoothness.

Blur an Image

Photoshop's Blur filters reduce the amount of detail in your image. You can use the Blur filters to apply a variety of blurring effects to your photos. The Gaussian Blur filter has an advantage over other Blur filters in that you can control the amount of blur added. The Motion Blur filter applies directional blurring, making objects appear to be moving. To blur a background behind an object, select the object using one or more of the selection tools and then invert the selection. See Chapter 4 for more on making a selection.

Blur an Image

1. Select the layer to which you want to apply the filter.

   To apply the filter to just part of your image, make a selection with a selection tool.

   Note: For more on layers, see Chapter 8. For more on the selection tools, see Chapter 4.

   (A) In this example, the glass bowl around the candy has been selected.

2. Click **Filter**.

3. Click **Blur**.

4. Click **Gaussian Blur**.

   The Gaussian Blur dialog box opens.

5. Click the **Preview** check box (■ changes to ☑).

   (B) A preview of the filter's effect appears here.

   (C) You can click 🔍 or 🔍 to zoom in or out.

6. Click and drag the **Radius** slider (🔲) to control the amount of blur added.

   You can also type a value in the Radius field.

In this example, boosting the
Radius value increases the
amount of blur.

7 Click **OK**.

Photoshop applies the filter.

TIP

How do I add directional blurring to an image?
You can add directional blur to your image with the Motion
Blur filter. This can add a sense of motion to your image. To
apply the filter:

1 Click **Filter**, **Blur**, and then **Motion Blur**.

2 In the Motion Blur dialog box, adjust the angle and
distance to customize the blur's direction and intensity.

3 Click **OK** to apply the filter.

Sharpen an Image

Photoshop's Sharpen filters intensify the detail and reduce blurring in your image. The Smart Sharpen filter has advantages over some of the other Sharpen filters in that you can control the amount of sharpening you apply. You can use the Sharpen filters to sharpen an image suffering from focus problems. You can also use the Sharpen filters to draw focus to part of an image. To sharpen only a part of your image, first select that part with one or more of the selection tools. For more on Photoshop's selection tools, see Chapter 4.

Sharpen an Image

1 Select the layer to which you want to apply the filter.

In this example, the filter is applied to the flower layer.

To apply the filter to just part of your image, you can make a selection with a selection tool.

Note: For more on layers, see Chapter 8. For more on the selection tools, see Chapter 4.

2 Click **Filter**.

3 Click **Sharpen**.

4 Click **Smart Sharpen**.

The Smart Sharpen dialog box opens.

5 Click the **Preview** check box (■ changes to ☑).

Ⓐ A preview of the filter's effect appears here.

Ⓑ You can click 🔍 or 🔍 to zoom in or out.

Note: Previewing at 100% shows changes most accurately.

6 Click and drag the sliders (⬓) to control the amount of sharpening you apply to the image.

C Amount controls the overall amount of sharpening across the edges in the image.

D Radius controls whether sharpening is narrowly confined to edges in the image (low Radius setting) or added across the entire image (high Radius setting).

E You can optionally click **More Accurate** (▪ changes to ☑) to process the file more slowly but with possibly better results.

7 Click **OK**.

Photoshop applies the filter.

TIPS

When should I apply sharpening?
It is a good idea to sharpen an image after you enlarge it or apply other transformations because these operations can cause blurring. Applying the Smart Sharpen filter can also help clarify scanned images.

How can I remove a specific type of blurring from my image?
The Smart Sharpen filter gives you additional control over the sharpening applied to your image. You can specify that it remove blurring applied by the Gaussian Blur, Lens Blur, or Motion Blur filter. To access it, click **Filter**, **Sharpen**, and **Smart Sharpen**. You can also add blurring in the first place as a Smart Filter, which gives you the option of removing the filter later.

Distort an Image

Photoshop's Distort filters stretch and squeeze areas of your image. For example, the Spherize filter produces a funhouse effect, making your image look like it is being reflected in a mirrored sphere. The Twirl filter turns the image into a swirl of colors, and the Ripple filter adds wavelike effects. The Shear filter enables you to tilt your image at an angle.

You can also distort an image by using the Distort command, located under the Edit menu. See Chapter 5 for more.

Distort an Image

1 Select the layer to which you want to apply the filter.

To apply the filter to just part of your image, make a selection with a selection tool.

Note: For more on layers, see Chapter 8. For more on the selection tools, see Chapter 4.

Ⓐ In this example, a glass dome in its own layer is selected.

2 Click **Filter**.

3 Click **Distort**.

4 Click **Spherize**.

The Spherize dialog box opens.

Ⓑ A preview of the filter's effect appears here.

Ⓒ You can click 🔍 or 🔍 to zoom in or out.

5 Click and drag the **Amount** slider (▦) to control the amount of distortion added.

In this example, the amount of the spherize effect has been decreased.

6 Click **OK**.

Photoshop applies the filter.

TIPS

What happens when I type a negative value in the Amount field of the Spherize dialog box?
A negative value squeezes the shapes in your image instead of expanding them. The Pinch filter — which you can also find under the Filter and Distort menu selections — produces a similar effect.

How can I quickly add wild special effects to my images?
Many of the filters in the Stylize menu produce out-of-this-world effects. The Emboss and Solarize filters are two examples. Click **Filter** and then click **Stylize** to access them.

Add Noise to an Image

Filters in the Noise menu add or remove graininess. You can add graininess to your image with the Add Noise filter to reduce detail or add a static effect. You can adjust the amount of graininess added to control how much of your image continues to show through. Although photographers usually try to avoid graininess in their photos, the filter can be useful to apply an abstract texture to a scene. Some filters under the Noise menu, such as the Dust & Scratches filter, help remove extraneous elements from your image.

Add Noise to an Image

1 Select the layer to which you want to apply the filter.

This image has a single Background layer.

Ⓐ To apply the filter to just part of your image, make a selection with a selection tool.

Note: For more on layers, see Chapter 8. For more on the selection tools, see Chapter 4.

2 Click **Filter**.

3 Click **Noise**.

4 Click **Add Noise**.

The Add Noise dialog box opens.

5 Click the **Preview** check box (☐ changes to ☑).

Ⓑ A preview appears here.

Ⓒ You can click 🔍 or 🔍 to zoom in or out.

6 Click and drag the **Amount** slider (🔺) to control the amount of noise added. You can also type a value for the amount of noise.

7 Select the way you want the noise distributed (◯ changes to ◉).

The Uniform option spreads the noise more evenly than the Gaussian option.

In this example, the Amount
value has been increased.

⑧ Click **OK**.

Photoshop applies the filter.

Turn an Image into Shapes

The Pixelate filters divide areas of your image into solid-colored dots or shapes. The Crystallize filter — one example of a Pixelate filter — re-creates your image by using colored polygons. The polygon colors are determined by the distribution of the colors in the image. You control the size of the polygons with a setting in the Pixelate dialog box.

To apply a Pixelate filter to only a section of your image, select it first with one or more of the selection tools. For more on selecting, see Chapter 4.

Turn an Image into Shapes

1 Select the layer to which you want to apply the filter.

In this example, the image has a single Background layer.

To apply the filter to just part of your image, make a selection with a selection tool.

Note: For more on layers, see Chapter 8. For more on the selection tools, see Chapter 4.

2 Click **Filter**.

3 Click **Pixelate**.

4 Click **Crystallize**.

The Crystallize dialog box opens.

Ⓐ A preview of the filter's effect appears here.

Ⓑ You can click 🔍 or 🔍 to zoom in or out.

5 Click and drag the **Cell Size** slider (🔲) to adjust the size of the shapes.

You can also type a value for the size.

The size can range from 3 to 300.

In this example, the Cell Size value has been increased.

6 Click **OK**.

Photoshop applies the filter.

What does the Mosaic filter do?

The Mosaic filter converts your image to a set of solid-color squares. You can control the size of the squares in the filter's dialog box. Apply the filter by clicking **Filter**, **Pixelate**, and then **Mosaic**.

What does the Stained Glass filter do?

The Stained Glass filter converts small areas of your image to different solid-color shapes, similar to those you may see in a stained-glass window. A foreground-color border separates the shapes. You can adjust the thickness of the border, along with cell size and light intensity. Apply this filter by clicking **Filter**, **Filter Gallery**, **Texture**, and then **Stained Glass**.

Turn an Image into a Charcoal Sketch

The Sketch filters add outlining effects to your image. The Charcoal filter, for example, makes an image look as if you sketched it by using charcoal on paper. The Charcoal filter uses the foreground color as the charcoal color and the background color as the paper color. Changing these colors alters the filter's effect. For more on adjusting colors, see Chapter 7. Many of the other Sketch filters apply the foreground and background colors similarly. The Charcoal filter uses the Filter Gallery interface. For more on the Filter Gallery, see the section "Apply Multiple Filters."

Turn an Image into a Charcoal Sketch

1 Select the layer to which you want to apply the filter.

In this example, the image has a single Background layer.

To apply the filter to just part of your image, make a selection with a selection tool.

2 Click **Filter**.

3 Click **Filter Gallery**.

The Filter Gallery dialog box opens.

4 Click **Sketch**.

5 Click **Charcoal**.

Ⓐ You can also select a different filter by clicking ▾ in the right pane.

6 Click and drag the sliders (⊟) to control the filter's effect.

You can also type values in these fields.

Ⓑ You can close the middle pane by clicking ⊼.

On a Mac, you can close the middle pane by clicking ▾ (▾ changes to ▲).

7 Click **OK**.

Photoshop applies the filter.

In this example, the thickness of the charcoal strokes has been increased, and the Light/Dark Balance setting has also been increased.

C Photoshop uses the current foreground color as the charcoal and the current background color as the canvas.

Note: For more on choosing the foreground and background colors, see Chapter 6.

TIP

What does the Photocopy filter do?
The Photocopy filter converts shadows and midtones in your image to the foreground color in the Toolbox, and highlights in your image to the background color:

1 Follow steps **1** to **4** in this section, but in step **5**, click **Photocopy**.

2 Adjust the detail and the darkness of the filter effect.

3 Click **OK**.

Photoshop applies the filter.

Apply Glowing Edges to an Image

The Glowing Edges filter — one example of a Stylize filter — applies a neon effect to the edges in your image. Areas between the edges turn black. Other Stylize filters produce similarly extreme artistic effects. You can adjust the width, brightness, and smoothness of the edges to achieve a range of looks for your image. This lets you keep as much or as little of the edge detail as you want.

The Glowing Edges filter uses the Filter Gallery interface. For more on the Filter Gallery, see the section "Apply Multiple Filters."

Apply Glowing Edges to an Image

1 Select the layer to which you want to apply the filter.

In this example, the image has a single Background layer.

To apply the filter to just part of your image, make a selection with a selection tool.

Note: For more on layers, see Chapter 8. For more on the selection tools, see Chapter 4.

2 Click **Filter**.

3 Click **Filter Gallery**.

The Filter Gallery dialog box opens with the Glowing Edges filter selected.

4 Click **Stylize**.

5 Click **Glowing Edges**.

Ⓐ You can also select a different filter by clicking ▾ in the right pane.

6 Click and drag the sliders (▣) to control the intensity of the glow you add to the edges in the image.

You can also type values in the slider fields.

B You can close the middle pane by clicking 🔼.

On a Mac, you can close the middle pane by clicking ▾ (▾ changes to ▴).

In this example, the Edge Width and Edge Brightness values are increased to intensify the neon effect.

7 Click **OK**.

Photoshop applies the filter.

TIP

What is the Find Edges filter?
The Find Edges filter is similar to the Glowing Edges filter, except that it places white pixels between the edges in your image. Find Edges is a one-step filter, which means you cannot fine-tune its effects in a dialog box before you apply it. To apply the filter:

1 Click **Filter**.

2 Click **Stylize**.

3 Click **Find Edges**.

Photoshop applies the filter.

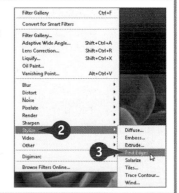

Add Texture to an Image

You can overlay different textures on your image with the Texturizer filter. The other Texture filters enable you to apply other patterns. Applying a Texture filter can make your image look like it is printed on canvas, or painted on a brick wall. Use the Canvas texture with one of the Artistic filters to make your image look like a painting on canvas. See "Turn an Image Into a Painting" earlier in this chapter for more on the Artistic filters. See "Apply Multiple Filters" in this chapter for information on applying both at once.

Add Texture to an Image

1 Select the layer to which you want to apply the filter.

To apply the filter to just part of your image, make a selection with a selection tool.

In this example, the filter is applied to a selection.

Note: For more on layers, see Chapter 8. For more on the selection tools, see Chapter 4.

2 Click **Filter**.

3 Click **Filter Gallery**.

The Filter Gallery dialog box opens with the Texturizer filter selected.

The left pane displays a preview of the filter's effect.

The middle pane enables you to select a different texture or another type of filter.

4 Click **Texture**.

5 Click **Texturizer**.

A You can also select a different filter by clicking ▾ in the right pane.

6 Click here (▾) to choose a texture to apply.

7 Click and drag the sliders () to control the scaling, or size, and relief, or intensity, of the overlaid texture.

You can also type values in these fields.

8 Click here (▾) to choose a **Light** direction.

B You can close the middle pane by clicking ▴.

On a Mac, you can close the middle pane by clicking ▾ (▾ changes to ▴).

9 Click **OK**.

Photoshop applies the filter.

TIP

What is a lens flare, and how can I add it to an image?
Lens flare is the extra flash of light that sometimes appears in a photo when too much light enters a camera lens.

1 Click **Filter**, **Render**, and then **Lens Flare**.

2 In the Lens Flare dialog box, click and drag to control the brightness.

3 Click and drag + to position the lens flare.

4 Click **OK**.

Offset an Image

The filters in the Other submenu produce interesting effects that do not fall under the other menu descriptions. For example, you can shift your image horizontally or vertically in the image window by using the Other submenu's Offset filter.

Selecting Wrap Around when offsetting an image enables you to create a seamlessly tiling background image for a web page or printed material. Selecting Repeat Edge Pixels when offsetting an image can give you an interesting and colorful margin where you can add text or other images.

Offset an Image

1 Select the layer to which you want to apply the filter.

In this example, the image has a single Background layer.

To apply the filter to just part of your image, make a selection with a selection tool.

Note: For more on layers, see Chapter 8. For more on the selection tools, see Chapter 4.

2 Click **Filter**.

3 Click **Other**.

4 Click **Offset**.

The Offset dialog box opens.

5 Type a horizontal offset.

6 Type a vertical offset.

You can also drag the sliders (⬚) to set values for the offsets.

7 Select how you want Photoshop to treat pixels at the edge (◻ changes to ◉).

8 Click **OK**.

252

Because a positive value was entered in the horizontal field, the image has been shifted horizontally to the right.

Wrap Around was selected in step **7**, so the pixels cropped from the right edge of the image reappear on the left edge.

In this example, the same offset is applied but with Repeat Edge Pixels selected in step **7**, which creates a streaked effect at the left edge.

TIP

How do I make a seamless tile?

1 Open an image that has even textures and coloring.

2 Perform steps **1** to **8** in this section to offset your image horizontally and vertically.

3 Clean up the resulting seams with the **Clone Stamp** tool (🔨). See Chapter 6 for details.

The resulting image tiles seamlessly when you use it as a web page background.

Using the Liquify Filter

Photoshop's Liquify filter enables you to dramatically warp areas of your image. The filter is useful for making objects in your image appear to melt. You can also use the filter to make subtle changes to edges of objects by pushing the edges in or out.

For a dramatic effect, or to warp a long edge or a large object, choose a large brush size. To work on a smaller part of your image or to achieve a more subtle effect, choose a smaller brush size.

Using the Liquify Filter

1 Select the layer to which you want to apply the Liquify filter.

In this example, the image has a single Background layer.

To apply the filter to just part of your image, make a selection with a selection tool.

Note: For more on layers, see Chapter 8. For more on the selection tools, see Chapter 4.

2 Click **Filter**.

3 Click **Liquify**.

The Liquify dialog box opens.

4 Type a Brush Size from 1 to 15000.

5 Type a Brush Pressure, or strength, from 1 to 100.

6 Click a Liquify tool.

This example uses the Forward Warp tool (🖉).

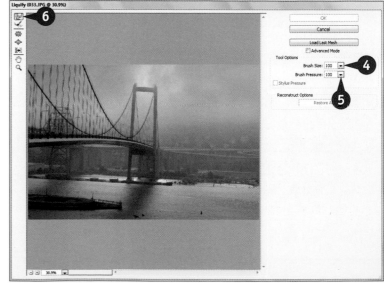

7 Click and drag inside the image preview box.

Photoshop liquifies the image where you drag the brush.

A You can click **Restore All** to change the image back to its original state.

8 Click **OK**.

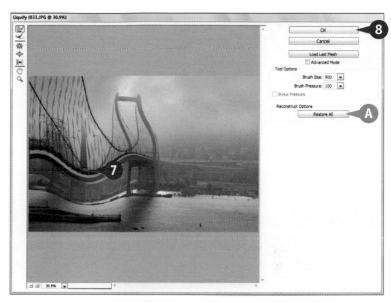

Photoshop applies the Liquify effect to your image.

TIP

What do some of the different Liquify tools do?

	Forward Warp tool	Pushes pixels in the direction you drag
	Reconstruct tool	Restores pixels to their original state
	Pucker tool	Pushes pixels toward the brush center
	Bloat tool	Pushes pixels away from the brush center
	Push Left tool	Pushes pixels sideways as you drag

Apply Multiple Filters

You can apply more than one filter to an image by using the Filter Gallery interface. The interface enables you to view a variety of filter effects and apply them in combination. Many filters open the Filter Gallery interface when you apply them, including Dry Brush, Charcoal Sketch, Glowing Edges, and Texturizer. See previous sections in this chapter for more on these filters. Not all the effects listed under Photoshop's Filter menu appear in the Filter Gallery.

Applying multiple filters enables you to create complex effects, including making your image appear to be painted with a brush on canvas.

Apply Multiple Filters

1 Select the layer to which you want to apply the filters.

In this example, the image has a single Background layer.

To apply the filters to just part of your image, make a selection with a selection tool.

Note: For more on layers, see Chapter 8. For more on the selection tools, see Chapter 4.

2 Click **Filter**.

3 Click **Filter Gallery**.

The Filter Gallery dialog box opens with the most recently applied filter selected.

The left pane displays a preview of the filtered image.

4 Click ▶ to display filters from a category (▶ changes to ▼).

5 Click a thumbnail to apply a filter.

Ⓐ The filter appears in the filter list.

6 Click the **New Effect Layer** button (⬛).

7 Click ▶ to display filters from another category (▶ changes to ▾).

8 Click a thumbnail to apply another filter.

B The new effect appears in the list.

You can repeat steps **6** to **8** to apply additional filters.

9 Click **OK**.

Photoshop applies the filters.

Note: The order in which multiple filters are applied in the Filter Gallery can result in different overall effects.

TIP

How can I turn off filters in the Filter Gallery?
Currently applied filters appear in a list in the lower right corner of the Filter Gallery. You can click 👁 to temporarily hide a filter in the list. A hidden filter's effects are not applied to the preview in the left pane of the Filter Gallery, nor are they applied to the image when you click **OK**. You can click 🗑 to delete a filter entirely from the list.

Using Smart Filters

Filters that you apply to Smart Objects in your images are known as Smart Filters. Smart Filters are *non-destructive*, meaning you can edit them and turn them on and off as you continue to make changes to your image. You cannot do this with filters applied to normal layers.

You can apply multiple filters in this way, and maintain control of each separately. For more on Smart Objects, see Chapter 8.

Using Smart Filters

Apply a Smart Filter

1 Select the Smart Object to which you want to apply a filter.

2 Click **Filter**.

3 Click a filter category.

4 Click a filter.

The dialog box for that filter opens.

5 Adjust the filter settings.

6 Click **OK**.

A Photoshop applies the filter to the Smart Object in the image.

B The filter appears in the Layers panel.

You can repeat steps **2** to **6** to apply multiple Smart Filters to the Smart Object.

Turn Off a Smart Filter

1 Click next to the Smart Filter.

changes to , and Photoshop turns off the Smart Filter.

You can click to turn the Smart Filter back on.

C You can click next to Smart Filters to turn off all the Smart Filters for a layer.

Edit a Smart Filter

1 Double-click a Smart Filter.

Photoshop opens the dialog box for the Smart Filter.

2 Edit the filter settings.

3 Click **OK**.

Photoshop applies the edited settings.

TIP

How can I control how a Smart Filter is blended with the Smart Objects in my image?

1 Double-click **Filter Blending Options** () next to a Smart Filter.

2 Click here () to choose a blending mode.

A You can click here () to control the strength of the applied effect.

3 Click **OK**.

Photoshop applies the Smart Filter with the updated blending.

Note: For more on blending, see Chapter 8.

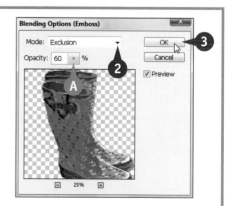

CHAPTER 11

Drawing Shapes

Photoshop offers a variety of tools for drawing geometric and abstract shapes. Other tools enable you to edit the lines that bound your shapes or change the colors with which the shapes are filled. You can also use the tools to draw lines that have arrowheads at their ends.

Draw a Shape

You can add solid shapes to your image by using Photoshop's many shape tools. These tools make it easy to add whimsical objects, labels, or geometric decorations to an image. You can also place frames around your photos or create buttons for your website.

Photoshop's shapes are *vector-based*, which means you can resize them without loss of quality. Shapes are usually placed in their own layer, and can be edited easily later on. See Chapter 8 for more on layers.

Draw a Shape

Draw a Solid Shape

1 Right-click the **Shape** tool (▣).

Note: The tool icon may differ, depending on the type of shape you drew last.

2 Click the shape you want to draw.

3 Click the **Shape Layers** icon (▣) on the Options bar and select **New Layer**.

4 Click the **Fill** box to select a fill color for the shape.

Note: For more on selecting colors, see Chapter 6.

5 Click and drag to draw the shape.

Photoshop draws the shape and fills it with the specified color.

Ⓐ The shape appears in a new layer in the Layers panel.

Note: For more on layers, see Chapter 8.

This example shows a shape being drawn on a new blank image.

Note: To create a new image, see Chapter 1.

Draw a Stylized Shape

1 Right-click the **Shape** tool and select the shape you want to draw.

2 Click here (▤) to open the style menu.

3 Select a style for your shape.

Photoshop offers a variety of colorful 3-D styles.

4 Click and drag to draw the shape.

Photoshop draws the shape and applies the specified style.

B The shape appears in a new layer in the Layers panel.

Note: For more on layers, see Chapter 8. For more on styles, see Chapter 9.

C You can move the shape by selecting its layer and then using the **Move** tool (▸⊕).

Note: For more on the Move tool, see Chapter 5.

How do I resize a shape after I draw it?

Click the shape's layer and then click the **Shape** tool (▨). Click **Edit**, **Transform Path**, and then a transform command. You can resize the shape just as you would a selection. See Chapter 5 for more on transforming selections.

How do I overlap shapes in interesting ways?

To determine how overlapping shapes interact, click one of the following options on the Options bar before drawing.

▣	Add to Shape Area	Combines a shape area with another shape area
▣	Subtract from Shape Area	Cuts a shape area out of another shape area
▣	Intersect Shape Areas	Keeps the area where shapes intersect
▣	Exclude Overlapping Shape Areas	Keeps the area where shapes do not overlap

Draw a Custom Shape

You can use the Custom Shape tool to draw a variety of interesting predefined shapes, including animals, frames, and talk bubbles. Photoshop comes with a variety of shape categories accessible from the Options bar. Custom shapes can be helpful when creating signs, banners, and other informational material. You can also use custom shapes as decoration when creating collages of your photos.

You can also apply styles to your custom shapes. See "Draw a Shape" for details.

Draw a Custom Shape

① Right-click the **Shape** tool (■).

② Click the **Custom Shape** button (■).

③ Click here (▾) to open the **Shape** menu.

④ Click the **Menu** button (⚙).

⑤ Click a shape category.

A dialog box opens to ask if you want to replace the current shapes.

Ⓐ You can click **Append** to append the new shapes to the current shapes.

⑥ Click **OK**.

Photoshop replaces the old shapes with your current shapes.

7 Click a shape.

8 Click the **Fill** box to select a color for the shape.

Note: For more on selecting colors, see Chapter 6.

9 Click and drag to draw the shape.

Photoshop draws the shape and fills it with the specified color.

B The shape appears in a new layer in the Layers panel.

Note: For more on layers, see Chapter 8.

C You can move the shape by selecting its layer and then using the **Move** tool (⊞).

Note: For more on the Move tool, see Chapter 5.

TIPS

How do I apply a shadow behind a shape?
You can apply a Drop Shadow style to the shape. Select your shape layer in the Layers panel and then click **Layer**, **Layer Style**, and **Drop Shadow**. A dialog box opens that enables you to customize the shadowing. For more on applying styles, see Chapter 9.

How do I overlay text on a shape?
You can click the **Type** tool (T), click your shape, and then type the text you want to overlay. This can be useful when you want to label buttons you create with the Shape tool. You should probably select a color for your text that contrasts with the color of your shape. For more on applying type, see Chapter 12.

Draw a Straight Line

You can draw a straight line by using Photoshop's Shape tool. You can point out elements in your image by customizing the line with arrowheads. If you press and hold **Shift** while using the Line tool, your line snaps to a perfectly horizontal or vertical plane, depending on which direction you drag the cursor. This can be a quick way to judge the layout of your image.

Lines can have arrowheads on one or both ends. You can customize the size of the arrowheads by specifying percentage values. The percentage values represent proportions of the line width.

Draw a Straight Line

1 Right-click the **Shape** tool (◼) and select the **Line** tool (◢).

Note: The tool icon may differ, depending on the type of shape you drew last.

2 Click the **Shape Layers** icon (◼) and make sure **New Layer** is selected.

3 Click here (⚙) to select the **Start** and/or **End** option (◻ changes to ☑) to add arrowheads to your line.

Ⓐ You can also specify the size and shape of the arrowheads by typing values here.

4 Press **Enter** (**Return** on a Mac) to close the menu.

5 Type a line weight.

You can use common units of measure, such as px (pixels), in (inches), or cm (centimeters).

6 Click here (▢) to choose a style for your line.

Ⓑ The Default style (▨) creates a plain solid line.

7 Press **Enter** (**Return** on a Mac) to close the menu.

Ⓒ You can click the **Fill** box to select a different line color.

8 Click and drag to draw the line.

Ⓓ Photoshop places the line in its own layer.

Note: For more on layers, see Chapter 8.

Ⓔ You can move the shape by selecting its layer and then using the **Move** tool (▸⊹).

Note: For more on the Move tool, see Chapter 5.

How do I draw a horizontal or vertical line?
Press **Shift** as you click and drag to create your line. You can also use this technique to drag lines at 45-degree angles.

How do I resize a line or another shape?
You can select the layer containing the shape, click **Edit**, and then click **Free Transform**. A bounding box appears around the shape. You can click and drag the handles (▢) on the sides and corners to resize the shape.

Draw a Shape with the Pen

With the Pen tool, you can create shapes by drawing the lines yourself. This enables you to make shapes not included in Photoshop's predefined menus. The Pen tool may seem difficult to use accurately at first, but with practice it becomes more natural and your lines become smoother. The Pen tool can be easier to use with a graphics tablet than with a mouse or a trackpad.

You can edit a pen-drawn shape just like you can a regular shape. See "Edit a Shape" for details.

Draw a Shape with the Pen

Using the Regular Pen

1 Click the **Pen** tool ( ).

2 Click the **Shape Layers** icon
( ) on the Options bar and
make sure **New Layer** is
checked.

3 Click the **Fill** box to select an
interior color for the shape.

Note: For more on selecting
colors, see Chapter 6.

4 Click inside your image to set
an initial anchor point.

5 Continue clicking to set
additional anchor points and
define the shape.

6 Click the initial anchor point
to close the shape.

Photoshop draws a straight-
sided shape.

Ⓐ Photoshop places the shape
on its own layer.

You can create curved paths
if you click and drag with the
Pen tool ( ).

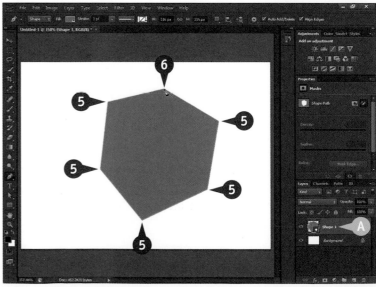

Using the Freeform Pen

1 Right-click the **Pen** tool (🖊).

2 Click the **Freeform Pen** tool (🖊) in the list that appears.

3 Click and drag inside your image.

Photoshop draws a free-form line.

4 Drag to the starting point of the line.

Photoshop completes the shape.

Alternatively, you can release the mouse, and Photoshop completes your shape with a straight line.

B Photoshop places the shape on its own layer.

TIP

How can I trace an object in my image with the Pen tool?

If the object has well-defined edges, you can trace it with the Freeform Pen tool (🖊) with the Magnetic option selected on the Options bar (☐ changes to ☑). The tool works similarly to the Magnetic Lasso tool (🧲). For more on using the Magnetic Lasso, see Chapter 4.

Edit a Shape

You can edit shapes by manipulating their anchor points. Anchor points are the draggable elements that appear at the shape edges and vertices when you draw the shape. You can add new anchor points with the Add Anchor Point tool.

Editing shapes lets you fine-tune their geometries. You can edit shapes drawn with the predefined shape tools or the Pen tool. Because shapes drawn with a Shape tool are vector-based, they remain smooth when edited. For more shape-editing techniques, see Photoshop's help documentation.

Edit a Shape

Move an Anchor Point

1 Right-click the **Path Selection** tool (⬛).

2 Click the **Direct Selection** tool (⬛) in the list that appears.

3 Click the edge of a shape.

Photoshop shows the anchor points that make up the shape.

4 Click and drag an anchor point.

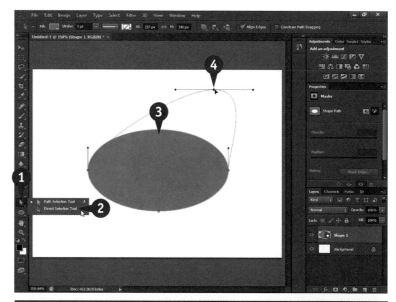

Photoshop moves the anchor point, changing the geometry of the shape.

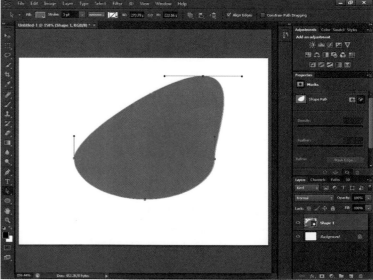

Bend a Straight Segment

1 Right-click the **Pen** tool (🖊).

2 Click the **Add Anchor Point** tool (🖊) in the list that appears.

3 Click a straight line between two anchor points.

Photoshop adds an anchor point to the line.

4 Click the anchor point and then drag.

5 Release the mouse.

Photoshop turns the straight line into a curved line.

You can use this technique to create a concave or convex curve.

TIPS

How do I edit curved lines?
If you click an anchor point on a curved line with the Direct Selection tool (▶), direction lines appear to the sides of the anchor point. You can click and drag the ends of the direction lines to edit the curve on each side of the anchor point. You can also click and drag the curves themselves with the Direct Selection tool.

How do I turn a shape layer into a regular layer?
You can turn a shape into a regular layer by *rasterizing* it. Click the shape layer and then click **Layer**, **Rasterize**, and **Shape**. After rasterizing, the shape's anchor points are no longer accessible. This means you cannot change the geometry of the shape by editing the anchor points. Most filter commands require you to rasterize a shape before you can apply the command to it.

CHAPTER 12

Adding and Manipulating Type

Photoshop lets you add type to your images and precisely control the type's appearance and layout.

Add Type to an Image

Adding text enables you to label elements in your image or use letters and words in artistic ways. You insert text in Photoshop using the Type tool. The Toolbox contains horizontal and vertical versions of the tool.

Text that you add appears in its own layer. You can manipulate text layers in your image to move or stylize text. Text in Photoshop is vector-based, so you can resize and transform it without a loss in quality. Photoshop comes with a number of expensive typefaces not typically preinstalled on computers.

Add Type to an Image

1 Click the **Type** tool (T).

2 Click where you want the new type to appear.

Note: You can also create a bounding box by drawing a shape. See Chapter 11 for more.

3 Use these menus to choose a font, style, and size for your type.

Note: To apply a shape by using type, you can choose a symbol-oriented font, such as Wingdings.

4 Click the **Color** box to select a color for your type.

Photoshop applies the foreground color by default.

Note: See Chapter 6 for more on selecting colors.

5 Type your text.

To create a line break, press
Enter (Return on a Mac).

6 When you finish typing your
text, click here (✓) or press
Ctrl+Enter (⌘+Return on
a Mac). You can also click
another tool in the Toolbox
to complete your text entry.

A Photoshop places the type
on its own layer.

B You can click the alignment
buttons to left-align (▤),
center (▤), or right-align
(▤) your type.

How do I create vertical type?

If you click and hold the **Type** tool (T), a list that contains
the Vertical Type tool (IT) appears. You can then use the tool
to create up-and-down type. When using the regular Type tool,
you can click the **Change Orientation** button (T) on the
Options bar to change horizontal type to vertical — and vice
versa. Note that with vertical type, lines go from right to left.

How do I reposition my type?

You can use the Move tool (▶) to move
the layer that contains the type. Click
the layer of type, click the Move tool,
and then click and drag to reposition
your type. For more on moving a layer,
see Chapter 8.

Add Type in a Bounding Box

You can add type inside a *bounding box*, which is a rectangular container for text, to constrain where the type appears and how it wraps. Adding text in a bounding box is useful when you want to constrain where the text appears in your image and when line breaks occur. You can change the dimensions of the bounding box by clicking and dragging handles on the corners and edges.

The bounding box remains the same size if you change how your type is sized or styled. See "Change the Formatting of Type" for details about changing how your type appears.

Add Type in a Bounding Box

① Click the **Type** tool (T).

② Click and drag inside the image to define the bounding box.

③ Click and drag the handles (□) of the bounding box to adjust its dimensions.

④ Click and drag the center point (⊕) of the bounding box to move the box.

⑤ Use these menus to choose the formatting for the type to be added.

6 Type your text.

Your text appears inside the bounding box.

A line of text that hits the edge of the bounding box automatically wraps to the next line.

Photoshop also automatically adds hyphenation.

Note: You can turn off hyphenation in the Paragraph panel. See the tip below for more.

7 When you finish typing your text, click here (✓) or press Ctrl + Enter (⌘ + Return on a Mac).

The bounding box disappears.

Ⓐ The type is put on its own layer.

Ⓑ To make the box reappear in order to change its dimensions, click the **Type** tool (🔳) and then click the text.

TIP

How do I format paragraph text inside a bounding box?

Follow these steps:

1 Click the **Type** tool (🔳).

2 Click the text inside the box.

3 Click **Window** and then **Paragraph**.

The Paragraph panel opens.

4 Type values or click the various tools to control the alignment, indenting, and hyphenation of the text inside the bounding box.

You can also format paragraph text with type styles.

Change the Formatting of Type

You can change the font, style, size, and other characteristics of your text. This can help emphasize or de-emphasize your text. Photoshop has access to all the fonts on your computer's operating system. A number of fonts are added when you install Photoshop.

Available styles for text include italic, bold, and other options that can vary depending on the font being used. The default size measurement is points, which are 1/72 of an inch. You can enter other units of measurement in the size field in the Options bar, such as "5 cm," and Photoshop converts the value to points.

Change the Formatting of Type

1 Click the **Type** tool (▥).

2 Click the type layer that you want to edit.

If the Layers panel is not visible, you can click **Window** and then **Layers** to view it.

3 Click and drag to select some type.

4 Click **Window** and then **Character**.

The Character panel opens.

You can also make many formatting changes on the Options bar.

5 Click here (▾) to open the font menu.

A Photoshop displays the names of available fonts.

You can turn on font previews in the Type preferences dialog box by clicking **Edit** (**Photoshop** on a Mac), **Preferences**, and then **Type**. Turning on font previews shows examples of each font in the font menu.

6 Choose a font.

7 Click here (▾) to choose the type's style.

8 Click here (▾) to choose the type's size.

9 Type percentage values here to stretch or shrink your type.

You can click other options in the panel to add more formatting.

10 Click here (✕) to close the panel.

11 When you finish formatting your text, click here (✓) or press `Ctrl`+`Enter` (`⌘`+`Return` on a Mac).

B Photoshop applies the formatting to your type.

TIPS

How do I edit the content of my type?
With the type's layer selected in the Layers panel, you can click the **Type** tool (**T**) and then click inside the text. Press `Del` to delete letters, or you can type new ones. You can press ←, →, ↑, or ↓ to move the cursor inside your type.

How can I check the spelling of my text?
Select your type layer in the Layers panel, click **Edit**, and then click **Check Spelling**. Photoshop compares your text with the text in its dictionary. It flags words it does not recognize and suggests replacements.

Change the Color of Type

You can change the color of your text to make it blend or contrast with the rest of the image. You can change the color of all or just part of your text. By default, Photoshop colors your text the current foreground color. For more about setting the foreground color, see Chapter 6.

You can also change the color of your text by changing the opacity setting of a text layer. Lowering the opacity of a layer makes it more transparent, and therefore makes text in that layer lighter in color and see-through. For more about changing opacity of layers, see Chapter 8.

Change the Color of Type

1 Click the **Type** tool (T).

2 Click the type layer that you want to edit.

   If the Layers panel is not visible, you can click **Window** and then **Layers** to view it.

3 Click and drag to select some text.

A You can double-click the layer thumbnail to select all the type.

4 Click the **Color** box on the Options bar.

The Color Picker dialog box opens.

5 Click a color.

B You can click and drag the slider () to change the colors that Photoshop displays in the selection box.

You can also type values for the color you want.

6 Click **OK**.

7 Click here (✓) or press **Ctrl** + **Enter** (⌘ + **Return** on a Mac).

C Photoshop changes the text to the new color.

TIPS

What is anti-aliasing?

Anti-aliasing is the process of adding semitransparent pixels to curved edges in digital images to make the edges appear smoother. You can apply anti-aliasing to type to improve its appearance. Text that you do not anti-alias can sometimes look jagged. You can control the presence and style of your type's anti-aliasing with the Anti-Aliasing Method (🔲) menu on the Options bar.

How can I apply a color gradient to my type?

You can apply the Gradient Overlay style to your type. Click the type layer and then click **Layer**, **Layer Style**, and **Gradient Overlay**. A dialog box opens, allowing you to define the gradient settings. For more on styles, see Chapter 9.

Warp Type

You can easily bend and distort layers of text by using the Warp Text feature in Photoshop. This can help you stylize your text to match the theme of your image. For example, text in a sky can be distorted to appear windblown.

Style options include Arc and Arch, which curves text in one direction across the image, and Flag and Wave, which curves the text back and forth across the image. Which direction the warping occurs depends on whether the warp is set to horizontal or vertical.

Warp Type

1 Click the **Type** tool (T).

2 Click the type layer that you want to warp.

If the Layers panel is not visible, you can click **Window** and then **Layers** to view it.

3 Click the **Create Warped Text** button (⬛).

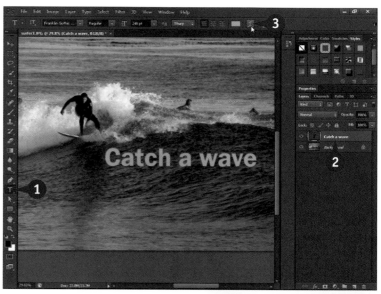

The Warp Text dialog box opens.

4 Click here (▾) to open the **Style** menu.

5 Click a warp style.

6 Click a radio button to choose an orientation for the warp effect (◉ changes to ◉).

7 Adjust the Bend and Distortion values by clicking and dragging the sliders (◨).

The Bend and Distortion values determine the strength of the warp. At 0% for all values, no warp is applied.

8 Click **OK**.

A Photoshop warps the text.

You can edit the format, color, and other characteristics of the type after you apply the warp.

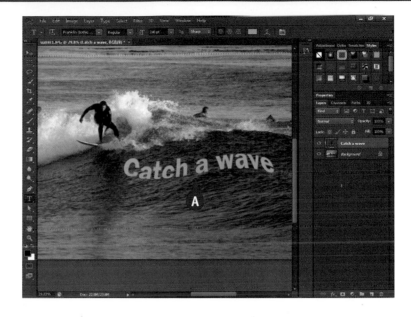

TIP

How do I unwrap text?

Follow these steps:

1 Click the **Type** tool (![T]).

2 Click the type layer that you want to unwarp.

3 Click the **Create Warped Text** button (![icon]).

4 In the Warp Text dialog box, click here (![icon]) to open the **Style** menu and then click **None**.

5 Click **OK**.

Photoshop unwarps your type.

CHAPTER 13

Automating Your Work

With Photoshop's Actions, you can automate repetitive imaging tasks by saving sequences of commands and applying them automatically to many image files. Other commands enable you to streamline your work by helping you create web photo galleries, picture packages, panoramas, and High Dynamic Range (HDR) images.

Record an Action

You can record a sequence of commands as an action and then replay it on other image files. This can save you time when you have a task in Photoshop that you need to repeat.

You can create actions that apply filters and styles, paint colors, and save files in specific formats. You can string together multiple commands to create actions that generate complex effects. After you record an action, you can play it. See the section "Play an Action" for more.

Record an Action

1 Click **Window**.

2 Click **Actions**.

The Actions panel opens.

3 Click a set in which to create your action.

Photoshop starts with a single set called Default Actions.

A You can click the **New Set** button (■) to create a new actions set.

4 Click the **Create New Action** button (■) to open the New Action dialog box.

5 Type a name for your action.

6 Click **Record**.

7 Perform the sequence of commands that you want to automate on your images.

B In this example, the first command, Auto Contrast, is performed by clicking **Image** and then **Auto Contrast**.

When automatically optimizing contrast, Photoshop performs a Levels adjustment.

Note: See Chapter 7 for more on adjusting colors and contrast.

C In this example, the second command is performed by clicking **Image**, **Adjustments**, and then **Desaturate**. This converts the image to black and white.

8 Click the **Stop** button (■) to stop recording.

D The Actions panel lists the commands performed under the name of the action.

What if I make a mistake when recording my action?

You can try recording the action again by clicking ▤ in the Actions panel and then clicking **Record Again**. This runs through the same actions, and you can apply different settings in the command dialog boxes. Alternatively, you can select the action, click the **Trash** icon (🗑) to delete the action, and then try rerecording it.

How can I control how fast the steps of an action are performed?

In the Actions panel, click ▤ and then **Playback Options**. A dialog box opens, enabling you to insert a pause after each step of an action. This can help you review the changes Photoshop makes to an image as it performs an action. The default behavior in Photoshop is to complete the actions as quickly as possible.

Play an Action

You can play an action from the Actions panel on an image. This saves time because you can execute multiple Photoshop commands with a single click. You can also play a specific command that is part of an action by itself. Photoshop comes with a variety of default actions already defined that you can apply to your image projects.

Actions that you record by using one image can be played on other images. See the section "Record an Action" for more.

Play an Action

Play a Full Action

1 Click **Window**.

2 Click **Actions**.

The Actions panel opens.

3 Click ▶ (▶ changes to ▼) to open an actions folder.

Note: To create your own action, see the section "Record an Action."

4 Click the action that you want to play.

5 Click the **Play Selection** button (▶).

Photoshop applies the action's commands to the image.

In this example, a sepia tone is applied to the image.

You can undo the multiple commands in an action by using the History panel.

Note: See Chapter 2 for more on the History panel.

Play a Command in an Action

1 In the Actions panel, click ▶ to reveal the commands that make up an action (▶ changes to ▼).

2 Click the command that you want to execute.

You can **Shift**+click to select multiple sequential commands.

3 **Ctrl**+click ▶ (⌘+click ▶ on a Mac).

Photoshop executes the selected command but not the commands before or after it.

In this example, the selected command adds motion blur to the image.

Note: To execute a specific command and all of those after it in an action, select the command and then click ▶ without pressing **Ctrl** (⌘ on a Mac).

TIP

How do I assign a special key command to an action?

1 Click 🔳 to open the Actions panel menu.

2 Click **Action Options**.

3 In the Action Options dialog box, click here (▾) to choose a key command.

4 Click **OK**.

To perform an action, press the key selected in Step **3**.

Note: Avoid assigning function keys already associated with a command. To view assigned key commands, click **Edit** and then **Keyboard Shortcuts**.

Batch Process by Using an Action

You can apply an action to multiple images automatically with Photoshop's Batch command. The command is a great timesaver for tasks such as optimizing large numbers of digital photos. You can also use the Batch command to apply the same special effect, such as adding a border or drop shadow, to a folder full of images.

To execute an action on a single image, see "Play an Action."

Batch Process by Using an Action

① Place all the images you want to apply an action to in a source folder.

② Create a destination folder in which to save your batch-processed files.

Note: To work with folders, see your operating system's documentation.

③ In Photoshop, click **File**.

④ Click **Automate**.

⑤ Click **Batch**.

The Batch dialog box opens.

⑥ Click here (▼) to choose an action to apply.

⑦ Click **Choose**.

The Browse for Folder (Choose a Batch Folder on a Mac) dialog box opens.

⑧ In Windows, click ▷ to open folders on your computer (▷ changes to ◢).

On a Mac, navigate to your source folder.

⑨ Click the folder containing your images.

⑩ Click **OK** (**Choose** on a Mac).

11 Click here (⊡) to choose **Folder**.

12 Click **Choose** and then repeat Steps **8** to **10** to select the folder where you want your batch-processed files to be saved.

Ⓐ You can specify a naming scheme for saving the batch-processed files.

13 Click **OK** (**Choose** on a Mac).

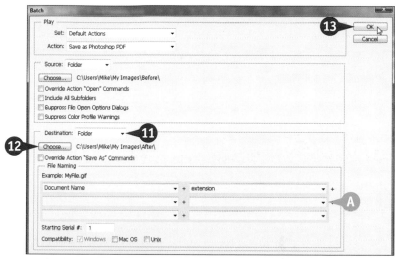

Ⓑ Photoshop opens each image in the specified folder one at a time and applies the action.

If the action includes a save step, Photoshop automatically saves each image in the destination directory.

Ⓒ If the action does not include a save step, Photoshop prompts you with a Save As dialog box for each image.

TIPS

How can I change the mode — such as RGB Color or Grayscale — of an image during a batch process, depending on its current mode?
When you record the original action, click **File**, **Automate**, and then **Conditional Mode Change**. A dialog box opens, asking you to specify the source modes that you want to switch as well as a target mode. When the action is run as a batch process, images of a selected source mode are converted.

How do I batch process by using an action in Mac OS X?
You do this very much like a Windows user does but with the Open dialog box rather than the Browse for Folder dialog box. When you click **Choose** in Step **7**, the Open-style dialog box opens. Using the file browser in the center of the dialog box, locate the source and destination folders for your batch-processed images.

Create a PDF of Images

Photoshop can automatically create a Portable Document Format (PDF) file that shows one or more of your photos. You can choose from a number of PDF templates, including ones for contact sheets and greeting cards.

You can view PDF files on your computer by using the free Adobe Reader. Download it here: http://get.adobe.com/reader. On a Mac, you can also use the Preview application.

Create a PDF of Images

① From Photoshop, open Adobe Bridge by clicking **File** and then **Browse in Bridge**.

Note: For more on accessing Bridge, see Chapter 1.

② Click **Window**.

③ Click **Workspace**.

④ Click **Output**.

Bridge displays panes for outputting images.

⑤ Make sure the PDF button is selected.

⑥ Click the **Folders** tab.

⑦ Click ▶ to open folders on your computer (▶ changes to ▼).

⑧ Click the folder containing your images.

The folder images appear in the bottom pane.

9 **Ctrl**+click (**⌘**+click on a Mac) to select the images you want to save in your PDF.

You can press **Ctrl**+**A** (**⌘**+ **A** on a Mac) to select all the images in the folder.

10 Click here (▼) to choose a PDF template.

11 Click **Refresh Preview**.

Ⓐ Bridge displays a preview of the PDF.

12 Click **Save**.

The Save dialog box opens.

13 Click here (▼) to choose where to save your PDF file.

14 Type a name for your PDF file.

15 Click **Save**.

Bridge saves your PDF and displays a confirmation dialog box.

16 Click **OK**.

TIP

What are some of the different customization options for PDF files in the Output pane?

- Document: These enable you to choose the paper size and orientation. You can also password-protect your file.
- Layout: These enable you to change the organization and spacing of the images on the page.
- Overlays: These enable you to display filename information over your images.
- Playback: These enable you to control how your PDF appears when viewed as a slide show.
- Watermark: These enable you to place transparent text over your images to indicate ownership or other information.

Create a Web Photo Gallery

You can have Photoshop create a photo gallery website that showcases your images. Photoshop not only sizes and optimizes your image files for the gallery, but also creates the web pages that display the images and builds the links and buttons that let you navigate the pages.

You specify the images you want to include in the gallery by selecting them from the Bridge interface. You can specify a gallery title and descriptive information to go with the photos.

Create a Web Photo Gallery

Build and Preview a Gallery

1. Place the images that you want to put into a gallery into a folder.

2. From Photoshop, open Adobe Bridge by clicking **File** and then **Browse in Bridge**.

Note: For more on accessing Bridge, see Chapter 1.

3. Click **Window**.

4. Click **Workspace**.

5. Click **Output**.

   Bridge displays panes for outputting images.

6. Click **Web Gallery**.

7. Click the **Folders** tab.

8. Click ▶ to open folders on your computer (▶ changes to ▼).

9. Click the folder containing your images.

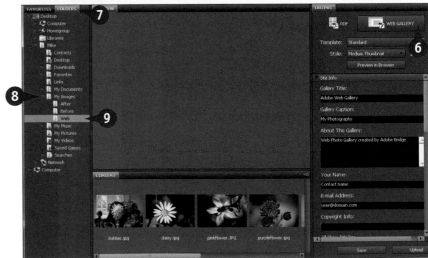

The folder images appear in the bottom pane.

10 Ctrl+click (⌘+click on a Mac) to select the images you want to display in your gallery.

You can press Ctrl+A (⌘+A on a Mac) to select all the images in the folder.

11 Click here (▪) to choose a gallery template.

12 Click here (▪) to choose a gallery style for your template.

The styles may vary depending on the template chosen.

13 Type a gallery title.

In most templates, this appears at the top of your gallery pages.

14 Type a caption and other descriptive information for your gallery.

15 You can type your name and e-mail address if you want people to be able to contact you through your gallery.

16 Click **Preview in Browser**.

TIPS

How can I customize the colors or layout of my photo gallery?
Under the Color Palette section of the Output pane, you can click color swatches to customize the colors of text, background, and other elements in your gallery. In the Appearance section, you can select the number of columns and rows as well as choose the preview size of the gallery images.

Do all the photo galleries require Adobe Flash?
Most of the Photoshop gallery templates make use of Adobe Flash to add interactive features. Viewers must have Flash installed in their web browsers to view these galleries. You can choose the HTML Gallery template in Step **11** to create a gallery based only on HTML, which means users do not need to have Flash installed to view it. Note that Apple iPhones and iPads cannot display Flash.

After you create your gallery, you can preview it in a web browser. Then, you can save it to your computer or upload it to a web server by using Photoshop's integrated File Transfer Protocol (FTP) client.

To upload your files to a web server, you need an Internet connection. You also need the username and password associated with your web hosting service. You web host can give you more information.

Create a Web Photo Gallery (continued)

Ⓐ Photoshop displays a preview of the gallery in your computer's default browser.

Ⓑ You can click links or thumbnail images in the preview to view larger-sized images.

Save to Your Computer

1 Click here (▼) to scroll to the bottom of the Output pane.

2 Type a gallery name.

Photoshop stores the files in a folder with that name.

3 Click **Browse**.

The Choose a Folder dialog box opens.

4 Select a location in which to save your gallery.

5 Click **OK** (**Choose** on a Mac).

6 Click **Save**.

C Photoshop saves the gallery in the specified location and displays a confirmation dialog box.

7 Click **OK**.

You can view the saved gallery on your computer by opening the gallery folder and then opening the index.html file in a web browser.

Upload to the Web

1 Type a gallery name.

Photoshop uploads the files to a folder with that name.

2 Type the login information for the FTP server.

You can check with your Internet service provider (ISP) for this information.

3 To upload your gallery to a specific folder, type the folder name here.

4 Click **Upload**.

Photoshop uploads the gallery files.

How can I save my FTP settings?

After you type your username, password, and other settings in the Upload section, you can save the settings as a preset by clicking ▣. The New Preset dialog box opens, and you can name your preset. Your saved presets can be selected from the menu in the Upload section. To delete a saved preset, select it from the menu and then click 🗑.

How can I change the behavior of the panels in the Output pane?

You can click **Edit** and then **Preferences** to open the Preferences dialog box. Then, you can click **Output**. If you click the **Use Solo Mode for Output Panel Behavior** check box, only one of the secondary panels in the Output pane will be active at a time. This is convenient if you would rather click headings to access the output options instead of scrolling.

Create a Panoramic Image

You can use the Photomerge feature in Photoshop to stitch several images together into a single panoramic image. This enables you to capture more scenery than is usually possible in a regular photograph.

Photoshop gives you stitching options to help ensure that your photos are combined appropriately. The final panoramic image can be relatively large. For tips on how to resize your image, see Chapter 3.

Create a Panoramic Image

1 Click **File**.

2 Click **Automate**.

3 Click **Photomerge**.

The Photomerge dialog box opens.

4 Click the **Auto** radio button (⊙ changes to ◉).

With the Auto setting, Photoshop automatically chooses the best method for stitching your photos together.

5 Click **Browse**.

The Open dialog box opens.

6 Click here (▾) to choose the folder that contains the images you want to merge.

7 Ctrl +click (⌘+click on a Mac) the images you want to merge into a panoramic image.

8 Click **OK**.

Ⓐ The filenames of the images appear in the Source Files list.

9 Click **OK** to build the panoramic image.

Photoshop merges the images into a single panoramic image.

Ⓑ Parts of each image appear in separate layers in the Layers panel.

Note: For more on layers, see Chapter 8.

Ⓒ You can use the Crop tool () to remove extra space around the panorama.

Note: For more on cropping, see Chapter 3.

10 Click **File** and then **Save** to save the panorama.

TIP

How can I create photos that merge successfully?
To merge photos successfully, you need to align and overlap the photos as you shoot them. Here are a few hints. For more tips, see the Photoshop help documentation.

- Use a tripod to keep your photos level with one another.
- Experiment with the different layout modes in the Photomerge dialog box.
- Refrain from using lenses that distort your photos, such as fisheye lenses.
- Shoot your photos so they overlap at least 30%.

Create an HDR Image

An HDR image is a composite image created from several photographs of the same scene, with each photograph having a different exposure. Photoshop combines the best lighting from each image to produce a single balanced image.

HDR images are good for scenes that have both light areas and dark areas. With the HDR feature, you can have details in both areas stand out, instead of having dark areas too shadowy or light areas too bright. HDR stands for *High Dynamic Range*.

Create an HDR Image

1 Click **File**.

2 Click **Automate**.

3 Click **Merge to HDR Pro**.

The Merge to HDR Pro dialog box opens.

4 Click **Browse**.

The Open dialog box opens.

5 Click here (▾) to choose the folder that contains the images you want to merge.

6 Ctrl +click (⌘+click on a Mac) the images you want to merge into an HDR image.

7 Click **Open**.

8 Click **OK** in the Merge to HDR Pro dialog box.

A Photoshop processes the images, merging their exposures and creating a single image.

9 You can click here (▾) to choose the method by which Photoshop adjusts exposures.

10 For the Local Adaptation and Exposure and Gamma methods, you can click and drag the sliders (▣) to fine-tune the lighting and colors.

11 Click **OK**.

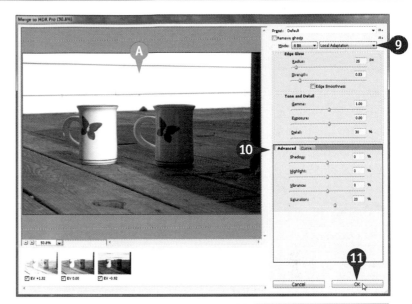

Photoshop displays the HDR image.

B In this example, tones for the lighter part of the image are taken from the source image with the shorter exposure.

C The tones for the darker part of the image are taken from the source image with the longer exposure.

How can I create source photos to use for my HDR image?

To create a good HDR image, you need several photos of the same scene, with each photo shot at a different exposure. Here are a few tips:

- Use a tripod to help ensure the content in your photos is aligned. A cable release can also help keep your camera steady between shots.
- When adjusting your camera settings, change the shutter speed rather than the aperture. This results in different exposures without changing the depth of field.
- If your camera offers it, you can use Auto Exposure Bracketing. This feature makes it easy to automatically shoot photos at several evenly spaced exposures.
- The more exposures you merge for your HDR, the more control you have over the tones in the resulting image.

Convert File Types

You can quickly and easily convert images from one file type to another in Photoshop by using the Image Processor script. This makes it easy to convert a collection of TIFF files to the JPEG format for posting on the web.

The Image Processor script enables you to convert to the JPEG, PSD, and TIFF file formats only. Another option if you want to convert images to a different format, such as PNG, is to create an action that saves a file in that format and then apply the action as a batch. See "Batch Process by Using an Action" for details.

Convert File Types

1 Place the images that you want to convert into a folder.

Note: To work with folders, see your operating system's documentation.

2 Click **File**.

3 Click **Scripts**.

4 Click **Image Processor**.

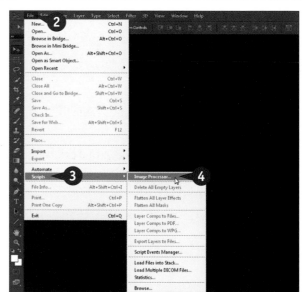

The Image Processor dialog box opens.

5 Click **Select Folder**.

The Choose Folder (Choose a Folder on a Mac) dialog box opens.

6 In Windows, click ▷ to open folders on your computer (▷ changes to ◢).

On a Mac, navigate to your source folder.

7 Click the folder containing your images.

8 Click **OK**.

⑨ Specify where you want your processed images to be saved.

⑩ Click an image file type check box (■ changes to ✓).

Ⓐ If you click **Save as JPEG**, you can also specify a quality setting from 1 to 12; the higher the quality setting, the larger the resulting file size.

You can click multiple format check boxes; Photoshop saves a separate image file for each format selected.

Ⓑ You can optionally click the **Resize to Fit** check box (■ changes to ✓), type a new width and height, and then Photoshop resizes the images before saving.

Note: Photoshop leaves the proportions of any resized images unchanged.

Ⓒ You can optionally click the **Run Action** check box (■ changes to ✓) to have an action executed on each image before saving.

Note: For more on actions, see the other tasks in this chapter.

⑪ Click **Run**.

Photoshop processes the images.

How can I quickly add the same copyright information to multiple images?
In the Image Processor dialog box, type the copyright information into the Copyright Info field. Photoshop adds the information to the processed images. To view the copyright information of an image in Photoshop, open the image, click **File**, and then click **File Info**.

How can I save my Image Processor settings so I can use them again later?
Click **Save** in the Image Processor dialog box. Another dialog box opens, enabling you to save the settings as an XML file. To load previously saved settings, click **Load** in the Image Processor dialog box.

Batch Rename Images

You can change the filenames of multiple images automatically with Bridge's renaming feature. You can customize the new name by using custom text, the date, sequential numbers, and more. You can copy or move the image files at the time that you rename them.

Renaming can be useful if you want to associate a large number of photos with a particular place, time, or person. Digital cameras typically name photos with incremental numbers, which is not very descriptive.

Batch Rename Images

1 Place the images that you want to rename into a folder.

2 From Photoshop, open Adobe Bridge by clicking **File** and then **Browse in Bridge**.

Note: For more on accessing Bridge, see Chapter 1.

3 Click the **Folders** tab.

4 Click the folder containing the images to rename.

5 **Ctrl**+click (**⌘**+click on a Mac) to select the images you want to rename.

You can press **Ctrl**+**A** (**⌘**+**A** on a Mac) to select all the images in the folder.

6 Click **Tools**.

7 Click **Batch Rename**.

The Batch Rename dialog box opens.

A By default, the renamed images are saved in the same folder.

B You can click the **Move** or **Copy** radio buttons (◯ changes to ◉) to save the images elsewhere. After you click Move or Copy, you can click **Browse** to select a destination folder.

304

8 Click here (▼) to choose a file-naming option.

9 Type in the text fields or choose from menus to customize the filename.

In this example, the images are renamed with an all-caps version of their filenames.

10 Repeat Steps **8** and **9** for other parts of the naming scheme.

C You can add or remove naming scheme options by clicking ⊞ or ⊟, respectively.

D An example of the new filename appears here.

11 Click **Rename**.

Photoshop renames the images in the folder.

TIPS

How can I rename images based on the camera settings they were taken with?
Choose **Metadata** for a filename option in Step **8** and then select a camera setting in the menu that appears. You can use aperture value, exposure setting, focal length, and other camera settings in your new filenames.

How can I save my renaming settings for use later?
Click **Save** in the Batch Rename dialog box. A Save As dialog box opens, enabling you to save the settings. To load previously saved settings, click **Load** in the Batch Rename dialog box.

Using Tool Presets

You can specify commonly used options for a tool and then save that set of options for loading and using later. For example, it can be helpful to define presets for brush styles and opacities you use often.

Photoshop stores the presets in the Tool Presets panel. You can keep this panel open as you work to have easy access to useful versions of your editing tools.

Using Tool Presets

Define a Tool Preset

1 Click a tool.

2 On the Options bar, specify the settings you want to save for that tool.

3 Click here ([▼]).

Ⓐ Previously defined and default presets are listed.

4 Click the **Create New Tool Preset** button ([▣]).

5 In the New Tool Preset dialog box, type a name for the tool preset.

6 Click **OK**.

Photoshop saves the tool preset.

Load a Tool Preset

1 Click **Window**.

2 Click **Tool Presets**.

The Tool Presets panel opens, listing the presets available for that tool.

Ⓑ You can deselect the **Current Tool Only** check box ([☑] changes to [■]) to display the presets for all the tools.

3 Click a preset.

⑥ The tool settings on the Options bar change to reflect those defined in the preset.

4 You can apply the tool to see the effects of the preset.

How can I easily manage a large number of tool presets?
The Tool Presets panel menu features a variety of commands for managing your presets.

1 Click [icon] to open the Tool Presets panel menu.

2 Click a command.

⑥ You can open the Preset Manager to view and organize your presets in a dialog box. You can also access it by clicking **Edit** and then **Preset Manager**.

⑧ You can save groups of presets as separate files on your computer and then reload them later.

CHAPTER 14

Saving and Printing Images

You can save your images so that you can use them in another application or on the web. You can also print your images to have a hard copy of your work. This chapter shows you how.

Save in the Photoshop Format

You can save your image in Photoshop's native image format. This format enables you to retain multiple layers in your image, if it has them. This is the best format in which to save your images if you still need to edit them. Because saving in Photoshop's native image format retains all of Photoshop's information about the image file, it results in a much larger file size than saving in a compressed format, such as JPEG or GIF.

Photoshop PDF and TIFF files also support multiple layers.

Save in the Photoshop Format

① Click **File**.

② Click **Save As**.

Ⓐ If you have named and saved your image previously and just want to save changes, you can click **File** and then **Save**.

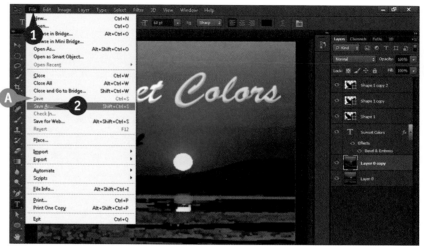

The Save As dialog box opens.

③ Click here (▾) to choose a folder into which to save the image file.

④ Click here (▾) to choose the Photoshop file format.

⑤ Type a name for the image file.

Photoshop automatically assigns a .psd extension if you do not specify an extension.

B To save a copy of the file and keep the existing file open, you can click the **As a Copy** check box (☐ changes to ☑).

C To merge the multiple layers of your image into one layer, you can deselect the **Layers** check box (☑ changes to ☐).

6 Click **Save**.

The Photoshop Format Options dialog box opens.

7 Click **OK** to make sure your image is compatible with other applications.

Photoshop saves the image file.

D The name of the file appears in the image's title bar.

TIP

What are the shortcuts for saving an image in Photoshop?
You can use several keyboard commands to save your image.

Command	Windows Shortcut	Mac Shortcut
Save	Ctrl + S	⌘ + S
Save As	Shift + Ctrl + S	Shift + ⌘ + S
Save for Web	Alt + Shift + Ctrl + S	Option + Shift + ⌘ + S

Save an Image for Use in Another Application

You can save your image in a format that can be opened and used in other imaging or page layout applications. If you are working with images which will be used in fliers or other printed material, you may need to use the TIFF or EPS format. TIFF (Tagged Image File Format) and EPS (Encapsulated PostScript) are standard printing formats that many applications on both Windows and Mac platforms support.

BMP, or bitmap, is a popular Windows image format. Most image formats — with the exception of Photoshop PSD, Photoshop PDF, Large Document, and TIFF — do not support layers.

Save an Image for Use in Another Application

1 Click **File**.

2 Click **Save As**.

The Save As dialog box opens.

3 In Windows, click here (⬇) to choose a folder into which to save the image file.

4 In Windows, click here (⬇) to choose a file format.

If you are saving a multilayer image and you select a file format that does not support layers, an alert icon appears. Photoshop saves a flattened copy of the image.

Note: See the section "Save in the Photoshop Format" to save a multilayer image. For more on flattening, see Chapter 8.

5 Type a filename.

Photoshop automatically assigns an appropriate extension for the file format, such as .tif for TIFF or .eps for EPS, if you do not specify an extension.

6 Click **Save**.

A dialog box opens with options specific to the format in which you are saving — the TIFF format, in this example.

7 Click **OK**.

Photoshop saves the image.

If a flattened copy is saved, the original multilayer version remains in the image window.

TIPS

What file format should I choose for my image?
It depends on how you will use it. If you want to preserve the layers of a multilayered image, save it as a Photoshop file or TIFF. If you want to use the image in word processing applications, save it as a TIFF or EPS file. If you want to use the image on the web, save it as a JPEG, PNG, or GIF file.

How can I save several images as a slide show presentation?
To create a slide show, you can save a selection of Photoshop images as a PDF in the Bridge application. See Chapter 13 for more. In the PDF Playback settings, you can adjust how the images appear when shown as a slide show.

Save a JPEG for the Web

You can save a file in the JPEG — Joint Photographic Experts Group — format and then publish it on the web. JPEG is the most common file format for saving photographic images. Many digital cameras also use it for saving their photos.

Photoshop saves JPEG images for the web at 72 dpi (dots per inch). When saving, you can adjust the JPEG quality setting to determine the file size of the resulting image. If you are saving a nonphotographic image, such as a line drawing or illustration, consider saving your image in the GIF or PNG-8 format.

Save a JPEG for the Web

1 Click **File**.

2 Click **Save for Web**.

The Save for Web dialog box opens.

3 Click the **2-Up** tab.

4 Click here to select the optimized version of your image.

5 Click here (☐) to choose **JPEG**.

6 Click here (☐) to choose a quality setting.

Ⓐ Alternatively, you can select a numeric quality setting from 0 (low quality) to 100 (high quality).

The higher the quality, the larger the resulting file size.

7 Check that the file quality and file size are acceptable in the preview pane.

B You can use the Hand tool (🖐) to move the image in the preview window.

C You can use the Zoom tool (🔍) to magnify the image in the preview window.

8 Click **Save**.

The Save Optimized As dialog box opens.

9 In Windows, click here (▼) to choose a folder into which to save the file.

On a Mac, use the Where pop-up menu or the File Browser to choose a folder.

10 Type a filename.

Photoshop automatically assigns a .jpg extension if you do not add an extension.

11 Click **Save**.

The original image file remains open in Photoshop.

TIPS

What is image compression?

Image compression involves using mathematical techniques to reduce the amount of information required to describe an image. This results in smaller file sizes, which is important when transmitting information on the web. Some compression schemes, such as JPEG, reduce image quality somewhat, but the loss is usually negligible compared to the savings in file size.

How can I optimize my web images to a specific file size?

In the Save for Web dialog box, click ▼≡ in the upper-right corner and then choose **Optimize to File Size**. A dialog box opens, enabling you to specify a target file size and other settings. Click **OK** to have Photoshop automatically select optimization settings to meet your requirements. The tool works with regular images and sliced images. For more on saving sliced images, see the section "Save a Sliced Image."

Save a GIF for the Web

Yଡ଼ou can save an image as a GIF — Graphics Interchange Format — file, and then publish it on the web. The GIF format is good for saving illustrations that have a limited number of colors. The GIF format supports a maximum of 256 colors.

Photoshop saves GIF images at 72 dpi (dots per inch). Unlike JPEG images, GIF images can include transparency. Transparency can allow images to appear as interesting shapes when displayed on a web page. If you are saving a photographic image with lots of continuous colors, consider saving your image in the JPEG format. See "Save a JPEG for the Web" for more information.

Save a GIF for the Web

1 Click **File**.

2 Click **Save for Web**.

The Save for Web dialog box opens.

3 Click the **2-Up** tab.

4 Click here to select the optimized version of your image.

5 Click here (⯆) to choose GIF.

6 Click here (⯆) to choose the number of colors to include in the image.

Ⓐ The Color Table displays the included colors.

GIF allows a maximum of 256 colors.

Ⓑ You can click here (⯆) to choose the algorithm Photoshop uses to select the GIF colors.

7 Check that the file quality and file size are acceptable in the preview window.

C You can use the Hand tool (🖐) to move the image in the preview pane.

D You can use the Zoom tool (🔍) to magnify the image in the preview pane.

E Clicking the **Transparency** check box (◼ changes to ☑) ensures that any transparent areas of your image remain that way in your final GIF image.

8 Click **Save**.

The Save Optimized As dialog box opens.

9 In Windows, click here (▾) to choose a folder into which to save the file.

On a Mac, use the Where pop-up menu or the File Browser to choose a folder.

10 Type a filename.

Photoshop automatically assigns a .gif extension if you do not add one.

11 Click **Save**.

The original image file remains open in Photoshop.

TIPS

How do I minimize the file sizes of my GIF images?
The most important factor in creating small GIFs is limiting the number of colors in the final image. GIF files are limited to 256 colors or fewer. In images that have just a few solid colors, you can often reduce the total number of colors to 16 or even 8 without any noticeable reduction in quality. See Step **6** in this section to set the number of colors in your GIF images.

How can I use GIF transparency in my web images?
GIF images that include transparency allow the background of a web page to show through. Transparent GIFs enable you to add nonrectangular elements to your web projects. Because Background layers cannot contain transparent pixels, you need to work with layers other than the Background layer to create transparent GIFs. See Chapter 8 for more.

Save a PNG for the Web

You can save an image as a PNG — Portable Network Graphics — file and then publish it on the web. PNG was devised as a higher-quality alternative to GIF.

Similar to GIF, PNG can support transparency, but PNG can support more than 256 colors. If you want to minimize the file size of a photograph, consider saving it as a JPEG instead because the JPEG format offers better compression, which results in smaller file sizes. See "Save a JPEG for the Web" for details.

Save a PNG for the Web

1 Click **File**.

2 Click **Save for Web**.

The Save for Web dialog box opens.

3 Click the **2-Up** tab.

4 Click here to select the optimized version of your image.

5 Click here (⬛) to choose **PNG-8** or **PNG-24**.

Note: See the tip at the end of this section for more on the different PNG settings.

318

6 Check the file quality and file size in the preview pane.

Ⓐ You can use the Hand tool (🖐) to move the image.

Ⓑ You can use the Zoom tool (🔍) to magnify the image.

Ⓒ Clicking the **Transparency** check box (☐ changes to ☑) ensures that any transparent areas of your image remain that way in your final PNG image.

7 Click **Save**.

The Save Optimized As dialog box opens.

8 In Windows, click here (▾) to choose a folder into which to save the file.

On a Mac, use the Where pop-up menu or the File Browser to choose a folder.

9 Type a filename.

Photoshop automatically assigns a .png extension if you do not add one.

10 Click **Save**.

The original image file remains open in Photoshop.

TIPS

What is the difference between the PNG-8 and PNG-24 settings?

PNG-8 stands for PNG 8-bit. With it, you can limit the number of colors in the final PNG image and thereby decrease the resulting file size. PNG-24 stands for PNG 24-bit. This format includes a wider range of colors than 8-bit and leads to better image quality but generally results in much larger file sizes.

How does the PNG format support transparency?

Like GIF files, PNG files can include transparency. But unlike GIFs, the PNG format supports a more advanced feature called alpha-channel transparency, which allows a background behind an image to show through partially. You can add partial transparency to your image by decreasing the opacity of a layer. For more on layers and opacity, see Chapter 8.

Add Descriptive and Copyright Information

You can store title, author, description, and copyright information with your saved image. You may find this useful if you plan on publishing the images online and want them to retain information about their source.

Some image-editing applications — such as Photoshop — can detect copyright information in an image and display it when the image is opened. Copyright laws give the creators of images certain rights to exclusively publish and distribute their works. Adding appropriate information to your images is one way to help protect your work.

Add Descriptive and Copyright Information

1 Click **File**.

2 Click **File Info**.

The File Info dialog box opens.

3 Type title and author information for the image.

4 Type a description for the image.

5 Type keywords for the image.

6 Click here (▾) to choose a copyright status.

7 Type a reference web address for the image.

8 Click **OK**.

A If you mark the image as copyrighted, Photoshop places a copyright symbol in the title bar.

To save the image, see the other tasks in this chapter.

How do I view information about a photo taken with a digital camera?

You can access information about photos taken with a digital camera in the File Info dialog box. You can view the information by clicking the **Camera Data** tab in the dialog box. The information includes the model of the camera, date and time the photo was shot, shutter speed, aperture value, and more.

What does Public Domain mean?

You can choose Public Domain from the Copyright Status menu to specify that your image is not owned or controlled by anyone and that the public is free to use it for any purpose. Marking something as public domain is in contrast to marking it as under copyright control.

Save a Sliced Image

You can save an image that has been partitioned with the Slice tool. Photoshop saves the slices as separate images and also saves an HTML file that organizes the slices into a web page. Slices enable you to save different parts of an image as JPEGs, GIFs, or PNGs. This can result in a smaller overall file size for the image.

When deciding what format to use for each slice, remember to consider how the slices will look as a whole. If some slices are compressed more than others, you could see a visible difference between parts of your page.

Save a Sliced Image

1 Open your sliced image.

2 Click **File**.

3 Click **Save for Web**.

The Save for Web dialog box opens.

4 Click the **Optimized** tab.

5 Click the **Slice Select** tool (▨).

6 Click one of the image slices.

7 Specify the optimization settings for the slice.

8 Repeat Steps **6** and **7** for each of the slices.

9 Click **Save**.

The Save Optimized As dialog box opens.

10 In Windows, click here (▾) to choose a folder into which to save the file.

On a Mac, use the Where pop-up menu or the File Browser to choose a folder.

11 In Windows, click here (▾) to choose **HTML and Images** as the file type.

On a Mac, click the **Format** pop-up menu (▾) and then choose **HTML and Images**.

12 Type the name of the HTML file that will organize the slices.

Photoshop saves the images by appending slice numbers to the original image name.

Ⓐ To change the naming scheme, you can click here (▾) to choose **Other**.

13 Click **Save**.

You can access the HTML and image files in the folder that you specified in Step **10**.

Ⓑ The image files are saved in a separate images subfolder.

Ⓒ To view the web page, you can double-click the HTML file. The file opens in a web browser.

Note: For more on using the Slice tool, see Chapter 4.

How do I publish my web page online?

After you create a web page by saving your sliced Photoshop image, you can make the page available online by transferring the HTML and image files to a web server by using an FTP program. Most people arrange for web server access through an Internet service provider (ISP).

How do I preview my optimized image in a web browser from inside Photoshop?

You can click **Preview** at the bottom of the Save for Web dialog box to open your optimized image in your computer's default web browser. Photoshop also lists statistics for the image, including the format, dimensions, and file size, in the browser window. After you preview the image in the browser, you can switch back to Photoshop to change the optimization settings or save the image.

Print by Using a PC

You can print hard copies of your Photoshop images on a PC by using an inkjet, laser, or another type of printer. You can then frame your photos or add them to a physical photo album. You can also print your images onto stickers, or onto transfer paper which can then be applied to shirts or other items. There are many options for creative ways to use your printed images.

You can preview your printout — as well as adjust the size and positioning of your printed image — before printing.

Print by Using a PC

1 Make sure the layers you want to print are visible.

Note: The visibility icon (👁) means that a layer is visible. For more on layers, see Chapter 8.

2 Click **File**.

3 Click **Print**.

Ⓐ To quickly print a single copy without previewing, you can click **Print One Copy**.

The Print dialog box opens.

4 Type a percentage in the Scale box to shrink or enlarge the image.

5 To print only a selected area of the image, click the **Print Selected Area** check box (☐ changes to ☑).

Handles appear around the page.

6 You can drag the handles (◼) to select the area to be printed.

7 Deselect the **Center** check box to allow repositioning of the image (☐ changes to ☑).

8 Click and drag in the image window to reposition the image on the page.

B You can position your image precisely by typing values in the Top and Left fields.

C You can click and drag the handles (☐) on the image corners to scale the image by hand.

9 Click here (▣) to choose a printer.

10 Type the number of copies to print.

11 Click **Print**.

Photoshop prints the image.

D You can click **Cancel** while printing is in progress to cancel the printing.

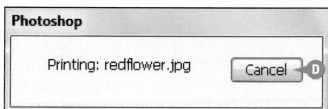

How can I maximize the size of my image on the printed page?
In the Print dialog box, you can click the **Scale to Fit Media** check box (■ changes to ☑) to scale the image to the maximum size given the current print settings.

How can I print my image on a page in landscape orientation?
Landscape orientation is when a rectangular piece of paper has its longer edge oriented horizontally. In the Print dialog box, you can click 🖻 to print in landscape orientation rather than the usual portrait orientation, which is with the longer side vertical.

Print by Using a Mac

You can print your Photoshop images in color or black and white on a Mac by using an inkjet, laser, or another type of printer. You can then frame your photos or add them to a physical photo album. Just as with a PC, you can print your images onto stickers, or onto transfer paper which can then be applied to shirts or other items.

You can preview your printout — as well as adjust the size and positioning of your printed image — before printing.

Print by Using a Mac

1 Make sure the layers you want to print are visible.

Note: The visibility icon (👁) means that a layer is visible. For more on layers, see Chapter 8.

This example has a single Background layer.

2 Click **File**.

3 Click **Print**.

Ⓐ To quickly print a single copy without previewing, you can click **Print One Copy**.

The Print dialog box opens.

4 Type a percentage in the Scale box to shrink or enlarge the image.

5 To print only a selected area of the image, click the **Print Selected Area** check box (☐ changes to ☑).

Handles appear around the page.

6 You can drag the handles (▼) to select the area to be printed.

7 Deselect the **Center** check box to allow repositioning of the image (☑ changes to ☐).

8 Click and drag in the image window to reposition the image on the page.

B You can position your image precisely by typing values in the Top and Left fields.

C You can click and drag the handles (□) on the image corners to scale the image by hand.

9 Click here (⬍) to choose a printer.

10 Type the number of copies to print.

11 Click **Print**.

A smaller Print dialog box opens.

D You can set printer-specific options from the pop-up menus that appear.

E You can optionally print to a PDF file by clicking here and selecting an option.

12 Click **Print** to print the image.

TIPS

What is halftoning?

In grayscale printing, *halftoning* is the process by which a printer creates the appearance of different shades of gray by using only black ink. If you look closely at a grayscale image printed on most black-and-white laser printers, you see that the image consists of tiny, differently sized dots. Larger dots produce the darker gray areas of the image, and smaller dots produce the lighter gray areas.

How do I save a group of printer settings on a Mac?

After specifying the settings for a print job, click the **Presets** pop-up menu, choose **Save As**, and then give the settings a name. You can access your saved printer settings in the Presets pop-up menu in the Print dialog box.

Index

055830328

Read Less–Learn More®

There's a Visual book
for every learning level ...

Simplified®

The place to start if you're new to computers. Full color.

- Computers
- Creating Web Pages
- Digital Photography
- Internet
- Mac OS
- Office
- Windows

Teach Yourself VISUALLY™

Get beginning to intermediate-level training in a variety of topics. Full color.

- Access
- Computers
- Digital Photography
- Dreamweaver
- Excel
- Flash
- HTML
- iLife
- iPhoto
- Mac OS
- Office
- Photoshop
- Photoshop Elements
- PowerPoint
- Windows
- Wireless Networking
- Word
- iPad
- iPhone
- WordPress
- Muse

Top 100 Simplified® Tips & Tricks

Tips and techniques to take your skills beyond the basics. Full color.

- Digital Photography
- eBay
- Excel
- Google
- Internet
- Mac OS
- Office
- Photoshop
- Photoshop Elements
- PowerPoint
- Windows

...all designed for visual learners—just like you!